Managing Institutions of
Higher Education
into the
21st Century

**Recent Titles in
Contributions to the Study of Education**

Rethinking the Curriculum: Toward an Integrated, Interdisciplinary College Education
Mary E. Clark and Sandra A. Wawrytko, editors

Study Abroad: The Experience of American Undergraduates
Jerry S. Carlson, Barbara B. Burn, John Useem, and David Yachimowicz

Between Understanding and Misunderstanding: Problems and Prospects for International Cultural Exchange
Yasushi Sugiyama, editor

Southern Cities, Southern Schools: Public Education in the Urban South
David N. Plank and Rick Ginsberg, editors

Making Schools Work for Underachieving Minority Students: Next Steps for Research, Policy, and Practice
Josie G. Bain and Joan L. Herman, editors

Foreign Teachers in China: Old Problems for a New Generation, 1979–1989
Edgar A. Porter

Effective Interventions: Applying Learning Theory to School Social Work
Eugene J. Meehan

American Presidents and Education
Maurice R. Berube

Learning to Lead: The Dynamics of the High School Principalship
Gordon A. Donaldson, Jr.

Windows on Japanese Education
Edward R. Beauchamp, editor

Integrating Study Abroad into the Undergraduate Liberal Arts Curriculum
Barbara B. Burn, editor

MANAGING INSTITUTIONS OF HIGHER EDUCATION INTO THE 21ST CENTURY

Issues and Implications

EDITED BY
Ronald R. Sims
AND
Serbrenia J. Sims

CONTRIBUTIONS TO THE STUDY OF EDUCATION,
NUMBER 48

GREENWOOD PRESS
New York • Westport, Connecticut • London

Library of Congress Cataloging-in-Publication Data

Managing institutions of higher education into the 21st century :
    issues and implications / edited by Ronald R. Sims and Serbrenia J. Sims.
        p.   cm. — (Contributions to the study of education, ISSN 0196-707X ; no.
    48)
    Includes bibliographical references and index.
    ISBN 0-313-27470-3 (alk. paper)
    1. Universities and colleges—Administration. I. Sims, Ronald R.
    II. Sims, Serbrenia J. III. Series.
    LB2341.M2785 1991
    378.1–dc20   91-22990

British Library Cataloguing in Publication Data is available.

Library of Congress Catalog Card Number: 91-22990
ISBN: 0-313-27470-3
ISSN: 0196-707X

First published in 1991

Greenwood Press, 88 Post Road West, Westport, CT 06881
An imprint of Greenwood Publishing Group, Inc.

Printed in the United States of America

∞™

The paper used in this book complies with the
Permanent Paper Standard issued by the National
Information Standards Organization (Z39.48–1984).

10 9 8 7 6 5 4 3 2 1

Contents

PART II
Academic Considerations

PART III
Service and Technology Management

Exhibits

Preface

> As houses are more or less livable, so books are more
> or less readable. The most readable books are an
> architectural achievement.... The best books are
> those that have the most intelligible structures.
> Though they are more complex than poorer books,
> their greater complexity is also a greater simplicity,
> because their parts are better organized, more
> unified.... The best books display a single unity of
> action, a main thread that ties everything together.
> — Adler 1986, p. 111.

In this book, that thread is a coherent and comprehensive
discussion of issues and practical action steps the reader can use
to determine what must be done to improve the college or
university. A well-written and useful book needs not only
coherence and comprehensiveness, it needs clarity. An important goal of this book is to steer clear of academic jargon,
pompous verbiage, lofty abstraction, and mathematical obfusca-
tion. It is our hope that all readers will view the writing in this
book as speaking of issues, threats, challenges, opportunities,
and solutions, and that each is anchored in concrete example
and detail. In sum, then, this book is intended to be practical —
a book that, through clarity and usefulness, invites its readers to
keep turning the pages. While any author is interested in high
sales, our primary goal is high readership.

The approach to analyzing educational management in times
of crisis and change taken in this book is both orthodox and
unorthodox, and also compelling, in that a variety of principles

will be applied to the higher education environment. This book offers the higher education community constructive discussions of higher education issues and action steps for colleges and universities facing challenging times.

The book is divided into three main parts: administration and internal governance, academic considerations, and service and technology management. These three areas generally are seen as those in which institutions of higher education focus their missions.

Part I, entitled "Administration and Internal Governance," contains articles that support the core college and university functions — the delivery of knowledge. These articles are arranged in a manner that will provide a cohesive understanding of some of the situations institutions of higher education will face as they approach the 21st century. The list includes academic leadership, the role of government, funding, and campus climate, which must respond to a plethora of issues.

Part II, entitled "Academic Considerations," contains chapters specifically related to bettering the primary focus of colleges and universities — the education of students. These articles center on the academic context of managing institutions of higher education: curricular innovations, student assessment, market-responsive educational programs, community college scholarships, and maximizing unit and individual performance.

Part III, "Service and Technology Management," includes chapters related to the service function and new technological considerations of colleges and universities. The chapters focus on the following areas: university research centers and technology transfer, university extension, and information management.

Managing Institutions of Higher Education into the 21st Century specifically addresses individuals directly responsible for managing institutions of higher education and should be read by federal and state legislators, educational foundations, boards of trustees, presidents, administrative associates, faculty members, students, and concerned lay persons, who ultimately must provide the energy and thrust for effective, efficient, and thoughtful entry into the future.

We thank James Sabin, executive vice president of Greenwood Publishing Group's series in Contributions to the Study of Education, and his staff. We especially thank Phyllis Viandis and Nancy Smith for assistance in typing earlier drafts of this book, along with Melissa Reagan, Carole Chappel, and Kim Wiseman for helping with endless and often last-minute copying requests. Most of all we thank all the contributing authors who found the time in their busy schedules to share their ideas.

Finally, we thank Nandi Rebeccah Cele and Dangaia Alfre Simone, who were most patient with us during our efforts to bring this book to fruition.

REFERENCE

Adler, M. J. (1986). *A guidebook to learning for a lifelong pursuit of wisdom*. New York: Macmillan, p. iii.

I

ADMINISTRATION AND INTERNAL GOVERNANCE

The University President: Academic Leadership in an Era of Fund Raising and Legislative Affairs

Lawrence Wiseman

Among U.S. institutions, higher education has long occupied a lofty position of public trust and confidence (for example, Harris, 1987, p. 256). Evidence suggests, however, that the university — described to me earnestly by one university president as "the last bastion of truth and honesty in this country" — is in danger of losing its special position of respect and privilege. Widely scrutinized athletics scandals, unappreciated tuition increases, sporadic research fraud, and consistent public attack by determined critics have all contributed to an erosion of public confidence in higher education (Palmer, 1988).

For an institution that relies on societal approbation — in alumni and corporate giving, foundation support, legislative favor, and the like — retaining public confidence is vital. If U.S. higher education fails to hold a respectful constituency, its economic, cultural, and scientific position surely will decline. Its vitality will be jeopardized.

Is there reason for concern? Maybe not. Steven Muller, recent president of Johns Hopkins University, believes today's universities "are great universities, greater than yesterday's" (1987, p. 705). Henry Rosovsky, former Dean of Harvard's Faculty of Arts and Sciences, adds "that fully two thirds to three quarters of the best universities in

This chapter is taken in part from the Seventh Annual Lecture on Higher Education and Public Policy, delivered by the author in April 1989, School of Education, College of William and Mary; and from interviews and correspondence with more than two dozen research university presidents in 1987–88 during tenure as an American Council on Education Fellow and Special Assistant to the President, University of Colorado. I especially thank presidents E. Gordon Gee, Paul R. Verkuil, and the others who work so hard and well for higher education.

the world are located in the United States" (1990, p. 29). But if U.S. colleges and universities are the best in the world, why do so many observers detect decreasing public support and trust?

There are two important possibilities: First, the university has become like any other business enterprise in the way it conducts and presents itself, losing in the process the special favor bestowed upon it by a respectful public. Second, the university presidency has been transformed in large part from an academic to a public relations position. These changes did not happen overnight, and they will not be reversed quickly.

The enormous number of books and articles crowding our offices and libraries (see, for example, the reference section at the end of this chapter) that detail higher education's perceived ills and offer prescriptive remedies for leadership, management, and planning suggest my point of view is not only simple-minded, but naive (and perhaps elitist). My defense is twofold: simple answers are often the best, and I am not so naive as to suggest either that universities abandon sound business principles or that presidents eschew skillful management and public relations practices in favor of the pure and narrow (that is, academics alone).

My point is simply that, as universities have become increasingly industrialized in outlook and operation, they slowly have given up what has served them well: the aura of integrity and special high purpose. Higher education must learn what televised religion has lately discovered about the consequences of altering public perception of mission and character.

Of course university leaders must manage their institutions properly. But they must also lead. Balancing the budget is essential, but so too is determining what that budget should support. It is not enough to insure institutional survival. The institution must stand for something. In order to appreciate what the institution can become, presidents must be of the university as well as for the university (Rosovsky's fourth principle to ensure reliable performance in university governance is "those with knowledge are entitled to a greater say" [1990, p. 269]). Therefore, the currently fashionable model of the external president surrendering meaningful academic involvement to the provost or vice president for academic affairs (who, in effect, becomes the internal president) should be discarded. Presidents must not abandon the academic arena in favor of the larger, public arena; they must, instead, bring the two arenas together. No one else can. As one president of a large university wrote: "Being able to communicate the academic enterprise to the outside world is a very fundamental responsibility of the president. Moreover, being able to interpret to the faculty the needs and trends of the larger society is also a very key role." Some faculty and presidents will consider this bad or useless advice. Others will consider it obvious.

THE UNIVERSITY AS A BUSINESS

Why is the university now seen by many as just another business? Maybe it's because "the never ending quest for money virtually overshadows all other tasks" ("Harvard's Helmsman," 1990, p. 54). The same public perception of yet another business is taking hold of both collegiate and professional athletics as well. Sports pages spend as much time considering pay checks, purses, and revenues as they do win-loss records and no-hitters. What was once the sporting life is now the business life. Escape from work has become work itself. In addition, big-time collegiate athletics further confuses university mission.

This image of bottom line accountability and responsibility in higher education is corroborated by a recent study suggesting that college and university presidents believe "maintaining a proper level of funding" is the most significant issue confronting higher education, more significant even than "ensuring the quality of academic programs" (Adams & Managieri, 1990). Recent articles in education journals proudly portray "The President as Salesman," and leave no doubt that presidents must be masters of marketing strategy and techniques (Hamlin, 1990). And a president's supreme success — overcoming financial crisis — is accomplished "by delegating academic and administrative duties to subordinates" (Hamlin, 1990, p. 13). The president takes over the truly important function of the university, raising funds, and leaves the less important academic duties to others.

But raising money does not define the university. The unique position colleges and universities have enjoyed in society derives in no small measure from their detachment, from their devotion to large questions and high ideals. They do not represent business as usual; they are not judged by profit margins. When the university behaves like any business, it is treated as any business. It loses some of its special character, some of its societal privilege. It loses distinction.

To recommend the university not act like a business suggests, perhaps, academic arrogance, but to suggest otherwise is to limit its potential as an institution of noble and transforming purpose. To fulfill its promise, the university must be inspirational as well as practical.

THE PRESIDENT AS FUND RAISER
AND ACADEMIC LEADER

In all aspects of university life, from athletics to zoology, the president is held responsible (see, for example, Thelin & Wiseman, 1989). It is not easy. Januslike, presidents must look forward and backward, they must look for money and for purpose. Can they do it?

George Keller (1983) laments that university presidents over the past few decades have become weaker as faculty, students, and other special interest groups have become stronger. While there is general agreement that university presidents do not have the power they once had (for example, Clark, 1987; Muller, 1987), still Clark Kerr suggests that "Virtually all successful major reforms or revolutions in the academic world have come into being and probably will continue to come into being through leadership from the top — or from the outside" (1982).

Newsweek magazine's "Conventional Wisdom Watch" asks, "Why don't college presidents cut the swath they once did? The answer: Maybe it's because, like politicians, they spend their days begging for money and covering their rears" (1990, p. 4). Such is the college president's dilemma. Success is measured by fund raising; fund raising leaves little time for leadership.

Robert Birnbaum refers to the presidency in his essay "Responsibility Without Authority: The Impossible Job of the College President" (1989). "Some presidents," he says, "spend a majority of their time in fund raising, public representation, and related resource-acquisition activities. The typical president spends little time on academic matters" (1989, p. 34). The president, operating in a complex and ambiguous setting (see especially, Cohen & March, 1974), is asked to be all things to all people. But the bottom line, more often than not, is raising money.

A president in whose tenure the university does not raise more money than it did before is a president looking for a new line of work. It is not surprising, then, that most presidents spend most of their time meeting with those individuals and groups that can help the university financially or that have influence. It is a necessary part of the job — and should be — and anyone who does not excel at it cannot make a good president. However, many presidents complain that while their capacity to lead is almost always, as one university president wrote, "based upon a record of academic credibility," fund raising and external affairs take up so much time that there is not enough left over for the academic agenda. In short, presidents do not have enough time to reflect thoughtfully upon the very things for which they are presumably gathering support.

THE PRESIDENCY AND THE LARGER VIEW

Former Duke University president Terry Sanford almost pleaded that "we need leadership in higher education to combat the growing apprehension that we do not know where we are going" (1977, p. 12). College and university presidents must play a fundamental role in the national education debate. They must be leaders. But as a popular news magazine reports, "Sadly, the rise of fund raising duties has diminished the impact of college presidents on the national scene. . . . The consequence: Fewer intelligent voices to debate pressing social issues" (Harvard's Helmsman," 1990, p. 54).

Of course a president must attend to matters close to home. Two most important institutional responsibilities are assuring survival and enhancing status. Both require public relations and developmental expertise, but both can also parochialize a president's efforts and effectively remove him or her from the national debate. What presidents do affects all of higher education, not merely their own institutions. They must use their skills and powers for all. Derek Bok, for example, has been an effective and constant voice not only for Harvard University, but for all of higher education. We need more presidents intelligently discussing the nature and needs of higher education publicly and within the halls of state legislatures and Congress.

Although I do not want to fall into Donald Walker's "Concept of the Heroic University Presidency" trap (1979), it does seem reasonable to expect presidents, as community leaders, to exert a more general, positive effect on higher education than they have done recently. Perhaps more cooperation and less competition is needed. At any rate, a more global public perspective from our university presidents can help restore luster to a somewhat tarnished image.

ARE PRESIDENTS AT FAULT?

If presidents are spending too much time raising funds and too little time raising issues, whose fault is it? Presidents have the ability and desire. Perhaps the problem is due partially to governing boards and faculties. Boards, often composed primarily of business people, may be more comfortable with one who speaks their language. Faculties may be more comfortable with one who does not interfere with their academic prerogatives. Both groups might prefer that the president stick with fund raising and stay out of the academic kitchen.

The university will fare better, though, if presidents are expected to be academic leaders as well as competent stewards of university resources. Academic leadership should not, by default, fall solely to provosts and faculties. As the only person within the university who interacts with every constituent group, the president must truly and deeply understand the nature of the university to be a persuasive advocate for it within these various and often conflicting special interest groups. Presidents must play the central role in defining the university's future and in setting institutional priorities:

The technical skills of the executive — reading balance sheets, estimating discounted present value or debt capacity, and similar arcana — are trivialities compared to understanding the fundamental nature of the university. And this has to come from inside experience acquired by long hours in library, laboratory, and with students (Rosovsky, 1990, p. 245).

This description of job qualification applies not only to deaning but to presidenting as well.

The president should understand that the product is obvious to the point of triviality, yet, the current rush to completely externalize the presidency seems acceptable to all concerned. However, the most important presidential role may be to help define what higher education should become in the next century. Questions of diversity, access, academic quality, assessment, cost, research, undergraduate teaching — all need active presidential involvement. Presidents will not find it difficult to attract competent people to help them raise money, but we must allow presidents the time to help set the course.

The good news is that maybe the tide is about to turn. Complex issues demand it. Perhaps "the crisis manager as president is likely to give way to the scholar/teacher; greatness awaits the master of that agenda" ("Giving Harvard Notice," 1990, p. 54).

REFERENCES

Adams, L. D., & Mangieri, J. N. (1990, Winter). The presidents: Priorities for the future. *Educational Record 71,* 8–9.

Birnbaum, R. (1989). Responsibility without authority: The impossible job of the college president. In J. C. Smart (Ed.), *Higher education: Handbook of theory and research, Volume II.* New York: Agathon Press.

Boyer, E. L. (1987). *College: The undergraduate experience in America.* New York: Harper & Row.

Clark, B. R. (1987). *The academic life: Small worlds, different worlds.* Princeton: The Carnegie Foundation for the Advancement of Teaching.

Cohen, M. D., & March, J. G. (1974). *Leadership and ambiguity: The American college president.* New York: McGraw-Hill.

Commission on Strengthening Presidential Leadership. (1984). *Presidents make a difference: Strengthening leadership in colleges and universities.* Washington, DC: Association of Governing Boards of Colleges and Universities.

Conventional wisdom watch. (1990, June 11). *Newsweek,* 4.

Fisher, J. L. (1984). *The power of the presidency.* New York: ACE/Macmillan.

Giving Harvard notice. (1990, June 11). *Newsweek,* 52–54.

Hamlin, A. (1990, Winter). The president as salesman. *Educational Record, 71,* 11–14.

Harris, L. (1987). *Inside America.* New York: Vintage Books.

Harvard's helmsman quits the race. (1990, June 11). *U.S. News & World Report,* 54.

Keller, G. (1983). *Academic strategy: The management revolution in American higher education.* Baltimore: Johns Hopkins University Press.

Kerr, C., & Gade, M. (1986). *The uses of the university* (3rd ed.). Cambridge, MA: Harvard University Press.

Muller, S. (1987). The university presidency today. *Science, 237,* 705.

Palmer, S. E. (1988, June 15). College presidents warned they must make changes of substance to avoid losing public's confidence. *Chronicle of Higher Education, 34*(40), A7.

Rosovsky, H. (1990). *The university: An owner's manual.* New York: W. W. Norton.

Sanford, T. (1977). Cooperative leadership. In R. W. Heyns (Ed.), *Leadership for higher education: The campus view.* Washington, DC: American Council on Education.

Thelin, J. R., & Wiseman, L. L. (1989). *The old college try: Balancing academics and athletics in higher education,* Report No. 4. Washington, DC: School of Education and Human Development, The George Washington University.

Walker, D. E. (1979). *The effective administrator: A practical approach to problem solving, decision making, and campus leadership.* San Francisco: Jossey-Bass Publishers.

2

The 21st Century University: The Role of Government

David Potter and Arthur W. Chickering

As we enter the 21st century, major societal changes will require dramatic departures from current organizational structures, curricular content, teaching practices, staffing patterns, and institutional priorities if universities are to be significant players in the world. Here are a few reminders of current U.S. trends and respected extrapolations.

WORK FORCE DEMOGRAPHICS

Between 1986 and 2000, the number of people aged 35–47 will increase by 38 percent, those 48–53 will increase 67 percent, and those 65 and older will increase by 150 percent to become 20 percent of the population. Total population growth will be only 15 percent (Johnston & Packer, 1987).

Minorities comprise an increasing proportion of the population. African-Americans, Hispanics and Native Americans, for example, represent one-fifth of the population today and will make up one-third within 20 years (Business-Higher Education Forum, 1988). More than half are being reared in poverty (Horowitz & O'Brien, 1989) and are ill-served by our school systems (Hamilton, 1988).

WORK PLACE CHANGES

Work requiring higher level skills in technical and service occupations will increase 50 percent by 2000 (Shostak, 1989).

Fifty percent of today's jobs will be replaced by new ones in the next generation (Shostak, 1989).

New technologies will be the dominant vehicles for information storage, transfer, and personal communication (Shostak, 1989).

Service occupations account for 71 percent of current employment and 68 percent of U.S. gross national product (Quinn & Gagnon, 1986).

About 100,000 U.S. firms do business overseas, including 25,000 with foreign affiliates and 3,500 major multinational companies; one-third of the profits of U.S. companies and one-sixth of the jobs are derived from international business (Cascio, 1986).

KNOWLEDGE AND SKILLS

Most persons can anticipate seven or eight lifetime jobs and three careers.

Demand for high skills in science, engineering, and medicine will double (Shostak, 1989).

Most available workers will come from minorities, disproportionate numbers of whom are dropping out of higher education.

An underclass is emerging in the United States. Nearly 15 percent of the population — 27 million people — may be functionally illiterate, unable to read the simplest information needed for daily life. In our cities, 44 percent of blacks, 54 percent of Native Americans, and 56 percent of Hispanic adults cannot read or write English at the eighth grade level (Business-Higher Education Forum, 1989).

U.S. businesses spend $210 billion for on-the-job training and education, about the same amount expended for public elementary, secondary, and higher education institutions combined.

These facts signify major changes toward an aging, multiethnic population trying to adjust to an internationalized, information-based economy and society. Higher education will have to cope with these developments and help resolve the problems they entail.

SHIFTS IN FEDERAL AND STATE ROLES

These changes have been accompanied by shifts in federal and state roles in higher education. Russell Edgerton, president of the American Association for Higher Education, describes the federal role this way:

There have been two major interventions by the federal government since World War II. The large dollar incentives for research caused a massive shift in emphasis which still persists. Most of these dollars have gone to major research universities. At the same time, as David Reisman tells us, backed by substantial research by Astin and others, it is really the private colleges which produce most of the good researchers; the research universities are not very good at producing their own. But this emphasis tends to drive the whole system, from institutional mission to faculty rewards. There are now about forty liberal arts colleges calling themselves "research colleges" in order to get under current federal funding guidelines.

The other major intervention was the decision to fund students instead of institutions, taken in the late 60's. This decision created the market factor. But it also had major consequences for federal support of higher education. Congress would probably not provide 1/20th of what it now provides if the decision had been made to fund institutions. The problem is that parents and students, the "market," are not very good levers for improving teaching and learning or for changing the system.

During the 1980s, federal spending increased 110 percent for research and development ($29.8 to $62.5 billion) and 94 percent for basic research ($4.7 to $9.1 billion). Most of this has gone for military- or defense-related projects, which increased from 50 percent to 70 percent of total spending. Federal support for nondefense research increased 59 percent, while support for defense-related research went up 191 percent. The proportion of federal research and development monies for university-based research fell from 14.3 percent in 1980 to 12.3 percent in 1988. In 1975 grants were 80 percent of student aid; by 1988 they were 49 percent. In recent years only 5 percent of state support is for need-based aid; 95 percent is a direct subsidy to all students.

While these changes were underway, the state role in regulation and budgetary control increased sharply. Statewide governing and coordinating boards became the major buffer among individual institutions, the legislature, and the governor, supplanting to a large degree the one-on-one lobbying that had dominated state dynamics before. Formula funding linked to institutional mission and grade level was adopted as the basic mechanism for allocating state dollars. New program approval became the major mechanism for controlling statewide redundancy and for monitoring institutional curricula. During the decade state initiatives, rhetoric, and limited dollars allocated to assessment, affirmative action, minority education, and centers of excellence have, at the margin, supplemented these basic roles.

As we enter the 1990s we are witnessing a withdrawal of government from its support of higher education. The privatization of higher education is proceeding apace, as the federal government devolves responsibility for a variety of governmental services to the states, and the states fail to accumulate the revenue needed to support these services. Faced with limited resources, state after state has taken actions that diminish the public's responsibility for higher education, imposing large cuts on the budgets of colleges and universities and passing on the burden of financial support to students and their parents.

These brief reminders about changes in society and higher education suggest some key characteristics for the 21st-century university. The Virginia Commission on the University of the 21st Century and an unpublished report on the impact of digital technology by Virginia Polytechnical Institute and State University (1989) suggest these basic ingredients:

The university will be a network of resources, not a place.

Offerings will give students a global, multicultural perspective.

Widespread use of new technologies will improve the quality of instruction, increase contact between students and faculty, and reduce constraints on time, place, and space.

Living and learning will be more closely integrated outside the classroom.

Teaching will be more responsive to individual differences.

Faculty roles, responsibilities, and rewards will expand and change.

Colleges and universities will be increasingly inter-dependent with other educational providers and the private sector.

Some of these characteristics advocated for the future are being developed on an experimental basis by enterprising individuals or institutions, but these observations and recommendations deserve more systematic consideration because they have sweeping implications for the future of higher education and for government's role in this enterprise. To address the implications for higher education we have adopted two complementary strategies. We have selected one overarching issue — the issue of boundaries — that cuts across many observations and recommendations, and we have taken a matrix approach to illustrate how we try to think about this subject.

The fall of the Berlin Wall is an apt image for this era. Old boundaries are disappearing, dismantled by aggressive attacks, eroded with age, collapsed under the weight of change. Dichotomies that were the building blocks for an industrial age are being replaced by new categories intended to capture this new world, and new metaphors are arising to capture the imagination and serve as guideposts to action. What now appears as social disintegration and fragmentation may be prelude to a new order. Higher education, and the governments that support it, must understand these changes and their implications for the future. Colleges and universities must participate in this transformation and use these changes to the betterment of education and society.

Exhibit 2.1 summarizes the changes now underway that signal a potential transformation within higher education. The changes are organized as a set of dimensions of higher education, each of which is experiencing boundary shifts: teaching and learning, the generation and organization of knowledge, the relationship between schools and colleges, the dynamics among institutions of higher education, national and international developments, and the contributions higher education makes to its society.

EXHIBIT 2.1
Boundary Issues: Impact on Higher Education

Teaching and Learning

Impact on Learning Boundaries

Learner as "partner with technology"

Break constraints of time and space — distance learning

"Classroom" redistributed throughout campus and beyond

Didactic pedagogy becomes interactive and facilitative pedagogy

Customized learning replaces standardized packaging

Nonlinear learning paths — "webs of knowledge"

Break lock-step equations of credit-for-contact and semester as unit of knowledge

Informal faculty-student relationships replace formal

Impact on Research Boundaries

Expanded information professional exchange networks

International networks of colleagues

New "webs of knowledge" generate serendipitous connections

Application and synthesis inform theory and method

Expanded research on learning and technology

New divisions of labor within professoriate — for example, noninstructional faculty

"Reflective" practitioners replace professional "experts"

Impact on Service Boundaries

Integrated library-computing information centers

Learning communities — networks of academic and nonacademic interest groups

Colearners replace professional experts and lay recipients of expertise

"Service" becomes integral with teaching and research

Impact on Organizational Boundaries

University distributed to urban villages and rural areas

Units become increasingly decentralized and autonomous

Departments and disciplines replaced by interdisciplinary centers and institutes

Joint learning ventures cross national boundaries

continued

Exhibit 2.1, continued

Increasing integration of academic programs and student services
12-month calendar; 7-day week; 18-hour day

Generation and Organization of Knowledge
Impact on Learning Boundaries
Overcoming "tyranny of the disciplines"
Interdisciplinary teaching and learning reflects knowledge frontiers
Diversity of learning "packages"
Faculty retraining
Precarious position of nonsponsored faculty research
Tension between professional and liberal education in curriculum
Thematic and problem centered curricular foci
Content plus competence
New degree programs in emerging fields
Impact on Research Boundaries
Frontier research creates new "disciplines"
Science and technology focus of R&D
Competitive knowledge development among university and nonuniversity research centers
Entrepreneurial uses of research
Collaborative, multi-institutional projects
Dispersed, global research networks
Impact on Service Boundaries
National competitiveness focus
Symbiosis of research and service in application of knowledge
Program developments with local or regional rationales
Community problem-solving teams
Joint ventures — R&D and product development affiliates
Impact on Organizational Boundaries
Privatization of research function
Collaborative research — government, nonprofit, private sector, and universities
Multidisciplinary centers and institutes
Research projects cross-cutting governmental agencies
Assessment of priorities for teaching and research
Intellectual property/profits rights issues
University/corporate degrees

Education and Schooling
Impact on Learning Boundaries
Linked curricula
Shared expectations for skill levels
Dissemination of pedagogical innovations
Overlapping transition zones
Joint enrollments
Impact on Research Boundaries
Student assessment
Clinical settings research
Study of student learning and developmental cycle
Impact on Service Boundaries
Community-based programs — for example, early identification

continued

Exhibit 2.1, continued

Teamwork to promote access — schools, foundation, and private support
Collegial ties between faculty, teachers, and other educators
Impact on Organizational Boundaries
"One system" — a "seamless web"
Sectors — integration, articulation
Alliances for joint projects
Higher education as system — interinstitutional ventures
Ties between higher education, "parasystems" and HRD in private sector
Shared faculty/practitioner faculty

Nation and the World
Impact on Learning Boundaries
Global perspective throughout curriculum
Manpower needs for new occupations — program innovations
Faculty development
Reconceptualization of course content
Satellite programs
World regions programs
Distance learning
Impact on Research Boundaries
Collaborative international projects — global and multinational issues
Applied research for national and international economic development
Concern for national security and secrecy — intellectual property
International data/researcher networks
Impact on Service Boundaries
International consultation and sharing
Scholar and student exchange programs
International internships for professional programs
Support for national competitiveness
Monitoring and advising on international developments
Impact on Organizational Boundaries
Internationalization of professional associations
Foreign ownership of colleges and universities
Partnership agreements with foreign institutions
Facilities established at sites abroad
Shared faculty appointments

Contributions to Society
Impact on Learning Boundaries
Basic skill development
Adapting the canon to multiculturalism
Preparing for the information economy and society
Values learning
Generic cognitive/affective/interpersonal competencies
Lifelong learning
Impact on Research Boundaries
National and international agendas for funding and support
International competition and cooperation

continued

Exhibit 2.1, continued

    Emphasis on applied R&D
    Environment and health issues
Impact on Service Boundaries
    Burgeoning demand for new services
    Leadership for community and nation
    Center for local and regional culture
    Joint programs for community development — partnerships with other sectors
    Retraining and contractual services
    Diversified services attuned to multicultural needs and providing access
Impact on Organizational Boundaries
    Interactive university
    Networks replace hierarchy
    Accountability demands
    Complex ties with other social institutions
    Creative financing of higher education enterprise
    Positioning supercedes planning

Boundary-breaking processes associated with each of these dimensions are altering the nature of higher education in teaching, research, and service and in the organization of colleges and universities. The complexity of these changes makes it difficult to elucidate each in the space available. We offer the figure as a concise way to capture this complexity. In the following text we do not aim to spell out all the information in the various matrix cells; instead, we aim to illustrate how we think about the interaction of these issues using this approach and to suggest the threads that weave through the details. For those interactions addressed in our illustrations, you are free to create your own text.

Teaching and Learning

Current standard instructional practices are artifacts of the industrial age. New technologies associated with the transformation to an information society offer opportunities for instructional innovation and new models for teaching and learning. Unlike earlier technological "fixes" for information transmission, these technologies are interactive and integrative. They enable networks of information and communication that overcome the boundaries of space and time. Hypertexts, for example, permit personal explorations of subjects that can take a student in uncharted directions, creating individualized "webs of knowledge" that can then be shared widely. Students can learn when and where they wish, transmitting questions and answers to teachers and others through electronic media, receiving instruction and feedback via the same mechanism. New forms of faculty-faculty, faculty-student and student-student interaction will result.

The boundaries for on-campus living and learning also can be blurred by distributing the academic enterprise to dormitories, student unions, and other sites traditionally peripheral to the learning experience. Beyond the campus, the same technologies permit distance learning, distributed throughout the emerging networks of "urban villages" to rural areas.

Faculty roles are also expanding to meet these needs. "Reflective practitioners" (Schon, 1983) are confronting the conventions of instruction and exploring the impact of integrative technology on course design and the teaching and learning process — including patterns of interaction between faculty and students and among students, feedback on student learning, and formats for assignments. Networks of faculty teaching the same subjects are forming, sharing course materials, making widely available the most up-to-date scholarship, and transforming research on teaching into learning experiments and new instructional approaches.

The "new scholar" will not only be a teacher and scholar, but will engage in discovery, application, synthesis, and communication, reaching wider audiences than students and professional colleagues, venturing regularly into the world at large (Boyer, 1990).

Generation and Organization of Knowledge

There is a subtle restructuring of knowledge in the late twentieth century. New divisions of intellectual labor, collaborative research, team teaching, hybrid fields, comparative studies, increased borrowing across disciplines, and a variety of "unified," "holistic" perspectives have created pressures upon traditional divisions of knowledge. There is talk of a growing "permeability of boundaries," ... even a profound epistemological crisis. To echo Clifford Geertz, there is indeed something happening "to the way we think about the way we think." These pressures have many origins and serve many purposes. However, they share one important commonality ... they have all been labeled interdisciplinary" (Klein, 1990).

Klein's work *Interdisciplinarity* describes experiments that undercut the distinctions between general and specialized education by combining disciplinary specialization with activities across disciplines. These experiments engage in problem-centered study that questions the sanctity of individual disciplines and professions and abandons traditional distinctions to study new subjects merging common features of related disciplines. The concepts of integration and collaboration permeate these innovations.

These experiments redefine boundaries of scholarship and learning, overcoming the "continuing rhetorical opposition of disciplinarity and interdisciplinarity" by recognizing that both "are not only relative to each other but also time bound in character" (Klein, 1990). In the process, these new forms threaten professional identities grounded in conventional academic life, forcing reforms in curriculum, in expectations of faculty, in competition for status within the academy, and in organizational alignments.

Much of the impetus for generating and organizing knowledge comes from the research enterprise. Recent developments blur the boundary between pure and applied research and challenge the primacy of academic research. The dominance of research and development, tied to corporate and national concerns with economic performance and potential, has stimulated a diversified research agenda and expanded the range of participants. The parameters of problem-focused, "field induced" issues, which cannot be subsumed within disciplinary or institutional categories, encourage new relationships among knowledge, action, and novel organizational arrangements to pursue these issues.

Education and Schooling

Indictments of U.S. schooling — the skill levels of its students, the preparation of its graduates for higher education, the profession of teaching, the participation and success rates of minorities — have inspired a belated recognition that schools, colleges, and universities share a common bond, the education of youth. In response educators are pursuing a variety of partnerships that break down the wall between secondary and higher education. The appeal for one system, an integrated and articulated educational enterprise, captures the theme of these innovations. These linkages, involving faculty beyond schools of education, establish new roles for both teachers and professors.

Alternatives to traditional schooling and higher education also are emerging. Joint ventures in corporate education and training by U.S. business and industry in cooperation with two- and four-year institutions are growing rapidly. Local school systems "have recently begun delegating financial and educational decisions to principals and teachers. Now the Dade County school system [for example] has extended this notion of site-based management to its logical conclusion: Let them design and run their own schools" (*New York Times,* 1990). Dade County invited not only teachers and administrators but also businesses and citizens to submit proposals for organizing its schools. Corporate foundations and corporations, seeking radically different approaches to education, have offered the financial incentives for these proposals.

Nation and the World

On the political front, events in Europe in 1990 made it abundantly clear that the world is undergoing a dramatic transformation. The dichotomies between East and West, between the Communist world and the free world, are obsolete. National boundaries are being challenged by subnational emancipation movements. Those who view the world as comprised of a set of national economies are being overtaken by the emergence of a global, interdependent economic system. Once again, technology has played a major role in these developments. Information conveyed by telecommunications media crosses national boundaries with impunity, rendering useless governmental efforts to control what is available to citizens and opening a new era of instantaneous communication with others. The information society is quintessentially a global village.

Higher education is responding to these revolutionary changes by redefining its involvement with the world beyond its borders. It is taking advantage of opportunities to develop new and expanded networks of relationships. It is being enlisted in support of national participation in the international arena. It is creating multinational research enterprises redefining its own perceptions of this new world within the curriculum.

Contributions to Society

For example, a recent publication (Business-Higher Education Forum, 1988), responding to concerns about the quality of education, calls for a revitalized system of higher education that will:

> restore a common sense of national purpose,
>
> affirm the dignity of work,
>
> recapture the belief in the future,
>
> rekindle a sense of values,
>
> cultivate our human resources,
>
> prepare and adapt U.S. workers to a changing world,
>
> nurture the talent of the people of the United States for creativity and inventiveness,
>
> cope with illiteracy, and
>
> incorporate minorities into society's mainstream.

Faced with an increasingly fragmented society, intensive international competition, and challenges to U.S. hegemony, society must turn to its colleges and universities for contributions at many levels.

Some institutions of higher education are responding by becoming self-consciously interactive, committed to work directly with business and political leaders of local, regional, and national communities. Programs are being developed that prepare students for life in the information society. Research is being conducted that applies to real-world problems. Partnerships are being established to sustain dialogue on community needs, offer joint services, and finance common enterprises that commingle educational and commercial activities. The classic ivory tower institution, walled off from town, is tumbling down.

The pace of change, which engenders perceptions of fragmentation and loss of purpose, makes decisions about how best to contribute to a complex society. Uncertainties abound, making conventional planning unsuitable. The recent emergence of chaos theory is a timely framework for an uncertain world, emphasizing as it does the nonlinear nature of complex systems and the potential impact of seemingly small changes.

Interactive colleges and universities strive to position themselves to respond to unanticipated changes and developments, to take advantage of opportunities that arise. The institution's orientation toward and interaction with its environment is more like a surfer than a hiker. The hiker selects a predetermined destination, lays out the route, estimates resources needed with some provision for unanticipated circumstances, loads the pack, and sets out. The surfer reads the waves carefully, waits for the right one, and then, with a delicate sense of timing and balance, sets out to ride just ahead of the wave. Once started the object is to stay upright and ride for maximum speed and distance. Success involves being in an intimate relationship with the environment, attuned to fast changing conditions. The destination is not critically important; what counts is making the most of that wave. Having done that, it is time to move back out and be ready for the next.

THE ROLE OF GOVERNMENT

The ability of U.S. higher education to assume a position of social leadership depends on political action at the federal and state levels, within executive, legislative, and bureaucratic offices. Each of the five boundary dimensions undergoing change is influenced by government's role. Exhibit 2.2 gives a set of recommendations for governmental actions that can support rather than impede these changes.

The proposals are organized under three kinds of governmental roles: *rhetoric*, by which governments and their agencies influence "the climate, attitudes and intellectual agendas or conceptions of the role and purposes of higher education"; *initiatives*, "working through incentives or sanctions to encourage or discourage particular policies and practices"; and *regulation*, "exercised through the processes for approving [and monitoring] institutional activities, missions, budgets and programs" (Chickering & Potter, 1990).

EXHIBIT 2.2
Boundary Issues: Impact on Government's Role

Teaching and Learning
   Rhetoric
      Call for pedagogical revolution
      Articulate vision of learning society
      Support distribution of learning throughout campus
      Charge institutions to establish joint learning ventures in communities and abroad
      Promote teaching mission
      Endorse "principles of good practice" for learning
   Initiatives
      Support instructional innovation
      Fund telecommunications infrastructure
      Sponsor research on learning styles and settings
      Create distance learning networks
      Convene and support networks of teachers and scholars
      Facilitate institutional cooperation to provide learning services
      Fund faculty development for individualized education
   Regulation
      Rethink "production line" guidelines
      Revise faculty work-load measures
      Reconceptualize categories of space needs and use
      Enable organizational changes that support interdisciplinary, decentralized or autonomous
         learning units
      Redefine concept of campus
      Support integrated alternatives to branch campus
      Change budget structure that separates instruction, academic support, and student services
      Revise staffing guidelines

Generation and Organization of Knowledge
   Rhetoric
      Challenge discipline dominance
      Preserve balance between professional and liberal education
      Define higher education's role in economic development
      Recognize knowledge as central resource for society
      Promote creation of full range of new knowledge, pure to applied
      Celebrate inventiveness and entrepreneurial spirit

continued

Exhibit 2.2, continued

Initiatives
    Support interdisciplinary learning and frontier research
    Facilitate collaborative research
    Fund faculty development to explore beyond disciplinary training
    Make available to faculty up-to-date data bases
    Provide financial incentives and rewards for research
    Sponsor applications of knowledge for community service
    Support curricular and research alternatives under Centers/Institutes
    Encourage certificate/credential and noncredential alternatives to supplement current degrees

Regulation
    Enable creation and implementation of degree programs in new disciplines
    Establish intellectual property guidelines
    Avoid excessive control of research
    Re-examine antitrust laws for R&D
    Monitor impact of entrepreneurial activity on educational mission
    Facilitate coordinated support of research across agency lines
    Develop sound policy for R&D activities
    Approve new programs that serve emerging local and regional needs

Education and Schooling

Rhetoric
    Establish "one system" vision
    Promote importance of education for 21st century world
    Encourage cross-sector staffing and teaching
    Emphasize the primacy of human resources for an information age
    Require articulation of skills needed for college level work
    Celebrate "model" programs

Initiatives
    Create cross-section programs
    Establish alliances among agencies
    Provide incentives for institutional cooperation
    Sponsor colloquia that convene broad range of educators to address common learning issues
    Convene school-college efforts to define appropriate skill levels by field
    Share information on pedagogy with teachers and other educators
    Fund research on student development cycle
    Support community-based programs
    Reinforce clinical professional education in school settings

Regulation
    Require information-sharing on student assessment across sectors
    Develop systematic articulation agreements
    Continue reform of teacher education
    Ensure student assessment for program improvement as well as accountability
    Establish new one-system governance and funding structures
    Assure access to higher education for all who can benefit

continued

Exhibit 2.2, continued

Nation and the World

Rhetoric

Articulate importance of global knowledge and perspective

Define higher education's role in balancing national and international interests

Establish national research teaching and curricular agendas and priorities

Initiatives

Support internationalization of curriculum

Increase research funding aligned with national and international agenda

Promote international projects

Establish accessible international information networks

Fund faculty and student exchange programs

Use faculty expertise on other cultures

Create international scholarly exchanges

Regulation

Approve new programs to infuse international elements in curriculum

Establish flexible guidelines to support partnerships abroad

Facilitate establishment of sites abroad

Evaluate impact of foreign ownership in higher education and U.S. investments in foreign sites

Contributions to Society

Rhetoric

Demand that higher education meet its responsibility for societal leadership

Articulate need for support of multicultural society

Define and disseminate information on skill and educational needs of knowledge-based society

Maintain awareness of need for access and educational success

Encourage recruitment and retention of stronger leaders

Initiatives

Establish state and national agendas for higher education in global world

Fund research and development to address social needs

Promote joint community development programs across institutional sectors

Support cultural activities for communities

Encourage joint degree/certificate programs

Assemble faculty and administrative leaders as participants on community problem-solving teams

Regulation

Approve programs developed in collaboration with community

Delineate new forms of accountability compatible with institutional autonomy

Re-examine institutional missions for the 21st century

Facilitate creative financing options developed in partnership with private sector

Provide incentives for expanded continuing education

Substitute initiatives for regulation to enable quick response to unanticipated change

---

The proposals in the exhibit are based on some underlying propositions that derive from our understanding of the developments and processes outlined above. The following text summarizes those propositions for the five boundary dimensions.

Our recommendations for teaching and learning reflect our belief that governments and their agencies should recognize that the conventions of instruction and the categories of bureaucratic planning are barriers to more effective learning. Self-conscious, shared reflection and study about learning must be undertaken by those engaged in the teaching enterprise where teaching and learning take place — in schools, colleges, and universities. These investigations must be related directly to each institution's own students and to the areas of knowledge, competence, and human development pertinent to that institution's mission.

Miami-Dade Community College has tackled this issue. Its Teaching/Learning Project, begun in 1986, has created a powerful mix of policy changes, concrete actions, and fresh resources. A steering committee, bolstered by subcommittees involving over 100 faculty members, have formulated recommendations for new, part-time and nonclassroom faculty, for classroom feedback and learning to learn, for faculty advancement and support, and for the role of administrators in supporting teaching excellence.

President Robert McCabe has convened collegewide small group meetings on faculty excellence and faculty advancement. The President's Council adopted recommendations to improve the teaching/learning environment. The college offers classroom feedback workshops and classroom research graduate courses, and 70 percent of participants are practicing new techniques to improve their teaching. Over two-thirds of the faculty voted to modify the institutional reward system to include improved teaching among the criteria for promotion and tenure. A publication to recruit new faculty includes a Statement of Faculty Excellence and a Statement of Teaching/Learning Values. Teaching/Learning Resource Centers, staffed by at least two professionals assisted by outside experts as needed, are placed on each campus. One hundred endowed teaching chairs are being established by corporate and individual donors (Miami-Dade Community College, 1990).

Other efforts like this are gathering momentum across the country. They need to be encouraged and facilitated by local, regional, and state governments so that all two- and four-year colleges can give priority to teaching and learning.

Governmental rhetoric, initiatives, and regulations must proceed from the realization that a knowledge-based society requires the vitality of good teaching and the good practices of active learning. Governmental actions must enable institutions to test and take advantage of new technologies that can be effective in the service of learning, to experiment and innovate, to replace antiquated practices and forms, and to radically reshape campus life.

Proposals for the generation and organization of knowledge argue for actions recognizing that the goal of research is to achieve a knowledge-based society and economy. This goal requires diverse forms of support. New arrangements will be needed to pursue knowledge, both within the academy and outside departments, and between higher education and other knowledge-generating institutions. Problem-centered research will overlap governmental agency lines and levels, requiring increased collaboration and coordination.

Georgia Institute of Technology, for example, has borrowed the land-grant model and applied it to engineering. Georgia Tech Research Institute houses an Industrial Extension Division, a statewide network of regional offices linked to the Atlanta campus, its experiment station, and the engineering faculty of the university. Each office is staffed by engineers who serve a range of industrial clients and technical needs. They respond to requests for assistance on problems, usually with projects involving manufacturing processes, facility and materials planning, methods improvement, or cost control. When regional agents do not have the expertise to solve a particular problem, they draw upon the research services of the institute. The mission of this system is to help small, technologically unsophisticated firms achieve greater economic and competitive equity by offering free service for several days and contractually negotiated services for longer projects. The state provides limited funding, and staff seek additional resources through contract work ("Georgia Tech Extension Model," 1990).

Suggestions for improved education and schooling call for actions that implement the concept of education as a seamless web for lifelong learning. This implementation must radically alter relationships among secondary schools, two- and four-year colleges and universities, and corporate human resources development. This requires greatly strengthened communication and coordination among educators and between educators and employers to avoid redundancy, increase efficiency and facilitate student transitions from one educational sector to the other.

The Institute for Educational Transformation (IET) in Northern Virginia that aims to find new answers to who teaches and who learns what, when, and where; to develop new structural relations among public, private, corporate, and professional institutions and individuals; and to strengthen the character of diverse educational partnerships. This collaborative effort includes the high-tech corporation IBM, a law firm, a venture capital business and a development corporation, a city council, city and county public schools, the local five-campus community college, and the regional university's school of education and its research and development center.

These partners establish the direction and evaluation of the institute; develop projects, proposals, and plans; implement agreed-upon projects; and disseminate knowledge of the institute's work. The first IET project, a $1.7 million effort funded in part by a grant from the U.S. Department of Education, involves the city schools, the city council, IBM, the development corporation, and the university research and development organization. Its initial focus is to bring together school science teachers, IBM scientists, science faculty from the university and the community college, and professionals from the development corporation. They will establish new staffing patterns and teaching locations and undertake to modify science education in the region.

Recommendations for the relationship between our nation and the world stress the globalization of economy, society, and knowledge. There is an urgent need to create educated citizens who understand other cultures and are able to participate in a multinational environment. Tensions between national and international interests need to be recognized and resolved. Students and faculty need firsthand opportunities for international experiences.

George Mason's International Institute is a concerted effort to strengthen the university's international activities and profile. Rather than seeking to establish a traditional school of foreign affairs, the institute is developing programs in selected areas, organized along issues or geographical areas, potentially inter-disciplinary and providing opportunities for interaction with external groups. The institute's Center for European Community Studies, founded in cooperation with the European Community, is a documentation center for the community, a resource for scholars and practitioners. It also is the administrative home for the European Community Studies Association, an international scholarly organization. The Center for Global Market Studies focuses on international finance and the G-7 process and related issues. International science and technology policy programs assess the influence of scientists and the advice they render on public policy, the interrelation between natural and social scientists in the development of public policy, and the role of research and development in industrial competitiveness. A master's program in international transactions provides a vehicle for students, mostly working professionals, to take advantage of these programs undertaken by faculty in collaboration with national and international partners. The Office of International Exchanges also helps students interested in studying overseas and assists the institute in establishing new ties with foreign institutions of higher education.

Propositions for education's contributions to society emphasize actions that require that higher education accept responsibilities for a broad range of community and national concerns. The rich human resources of higher education need to be employed systematically to accomplish the transition to a knowledge-based society while protecting student access and assuring solid outcomes in knowledge, competence, and human understanding. Government, higher education, and corporate partnerships will be needed to address social fragmentation and the creation of a multicultural democratic society.

The Center for Conflict Analysis and Resolution and the Conflict Clinic, housed at George Mason University and comprised of scholars, practitioners, graduate students, and organizations in the field of peacemaking and conflict resolution, are engaged in a partnership to address the conflicts associated with social fragmentation and multiculturalism. The mission of the center is to advance the understanding and resolution of persistent human conflicts among individuals, groups, communities, identity groups, and nations through research, instruction, and clinical and outreach activities.

CONCLUSION

During the last part of the 19th century, beginning with the Morrill Act in 1852, federal legislation and significant state support created the land-grant colleges that became the major vehicles for improving agricultural production and responding to the social changes provoked by the industrial revolution. There was widespread recognition that the prevailing model for higher education — small, private, mostly church-related colleges — though useful, was not sufficient to provide the skilled human resources, research, and technological assistance needed for that new age.

During the 1960s and early 1970s states and local communities, with some federal assistance, invested heavily in community colleges throughout each state across the country. Once again there was a powerful response to new social conditions. There was widespread recognition that the existing four-year institutions, and the sprinkling of junior colleges, though useful, were not sufficient to meet the needs for skilled workers and a more broadly educated citizenry. During the early and mid-20th century higher education had moved from an aristocratic orientation aimed at educating upper- and upper-middle-class men, to a meritocratic orientation aimed at educating the best and the brightest. By the 1960s the United States recognized the need for an egalitarian orientation that would make higher education accessible to all who could profit from it. Four-year institutions became more open, often simply revolving doors. A new institution was needed that would take seriously the need to provide useful postsecondary education to all who desired it.

Now the nation faces a similar challenge. Although existing two-year and four-year institutions, public and private, organized around traditional conventions concerning mission, content, campus, and calendar will continue to be useful, a new thrust in higher education is needed, similar in significance and scope to those that inspired the land-grant university and community college movements. Governments ought to play a major role in establishing and supporting this thrust, recognizing that a knowledge-based society requires the presence of viable, socially productive institutions of higher education. At present, it is unclear whether either the public or its political representatives understand the role that higher education must play in preparing us for the world of the 21st century. It also is unclear whether faculty and administrators at our institutions comprehend the systematic changes necessary to accomplish needed reforms and legitimize the new roles expected of them. The task is to create a viable vision of the 21st-century college and university; to mobilize educators, governments, and the public in support of that vision; and to create new coalitions across sectors to accomplish the vision. Failing that, higher education will be inadequate to serve the polity and unprepared for full participation in the global era.

REFERENCES

Arnett, E. C. (1989, July 20). Futurists gaze into business's crystal ball. *Washington Post,* pp. F1–F2.

Boyer, E. L. (1990). *Scholarship reconsidered: Priorities of the professoriate.* Princeton: Carnegie Foundation for the Advancement of Teaching.

Business-Higher Education Forum. (1988). *American potential: The human dimension.* Washington, DC: American Council on Education.

Cascio, W. F. (1986). *Managing human resources.* New York: McGraw-Hill.

Chickering, A. W., & Potter, D. L. (1990). Students, faculty, environment: State actions and institutional responses. In Peter Seldin (Ed.), *How administrators can improve teaching* (pp. 143–62). San Francisco: Jossey-Bass Publishers.

Commission on the University of the 21st Century. (1989). *The case for change.* Richmond, VA: The Commonwealth of Virginia.

Fiske, E. B. (1990, April 8). Starting over. *New York Times,* pp. 34–35.

The Georgia Tech Extension Model. (1990, May/June). *Change, 22*(3), 14.

Hamilton, M. H. (1988, July 10). Employing new tools to recruit workers. *Washington Post,* pp. H1, H3.

Horowitz, F. D., & O'Brien, M. (1989). In the interest of the nation: A reflective essay on the state of our knowledge and the challenges before us. *American Psychologist, 44,* 441–45.

Johnson, W. B., & Packer, A. H. (1987). *Workforce 2000: Work and workers for the twenty-first century.* Indianapolis: Hudson Institute.

Klein, J. T. (1990). *Interdisciplinarity.* Detroit: Wayne State University Press.

Miami-Dade Community College. (1990). *Summary report 1988–89.* Mardee Jenrette, Director, Teaching/Learning Project. Miami: Miami-Dade Community College.

Odiorne, G. S. (1986). The crystal ball of HR strategy. *Personnel Administrator, 31,* 103–6.

Quinn, J. B., & Gagnon, C. E. (1986, November–December). Will services follow manufacturing into decline? *Harvard Business Review, 64*(5), 95–103.

Schon, D. A. (1983). *The reflective practitioner: How professionals think in action.* New York: Basic Books.

Shostak, A. (1989, May). Keynote presentation at the meeting of the Council for the Advancement of Experiential Learning (CAEL) Assembly, Philadelphia.

U.S. Bureau of Labor Statistics. (1987, August). Press release (No. 87-345). Washington, DC: U.S. Department of Labor.

Virginia Polytechnic Institute and State University. (1989). *Report of the university task force on the impact of digital technology on the classroom environment.* Blacksburg, VA: Virginia Polytechnic Institute and State University.

3

Funding Reality within Higher Education: Can Universities Cope?

Norman J. Bregman and Micheal R. Moffett

U.S. society believes more is better and, therefore, a reduction or decline in any aspect of one's life is generally viewed as undesirable. Universities also tend to define success in terms of expansion. Since institutions do not think in terms of cutbacks or decline, those in the academy responsible for financial planning are very often unprepared to cope with this dilemma (Levine, 1978). However, the issues that insufficient funding produce are very complicated and multifaceted.

Administrators and faculties of institutions of higher education are facing the reality of decline or insufficient financial resources to operate university programs. These aspects of decline include a decreasing pool of traditional-aged college students (18- to 22-year-olds), a changed campus environment where administrators and faculty have to be sensitive to the needs (psychological and financial) of nontraditional individuals, recruiting wars to hold enrollment steady, increasing operating and maintenance costs, obsolete instructional and scientific equipment, deferred maintenance, diminished government support, and a growing shortage of qualified professionals for the available faculty spots. Any of the afore-mentioned issues alone would create significant problems for higher education, but linked and intertwined they present unprecedented problems for its administration.

Institutions of higher learning are confronted with declining or insufficient revenue in a period of spiraling costs for goods and services. Legislators have been unwilling to provide the necessary funds because of pressures to hold the line on taxes. Athletic programs have placed an added strain on limited financial resources. This problem has been exacerbated by the quest to be the best in all university areas of operation in order to recruit and retain outstanding students.

"Quality" has become the buzz word universities use to attract students and donations from alumni and friends during development drives. This compelling force to be noticed, to be number one, has driven institutions of higher learning to seek expertise in major campaigns of fund raising and marketing techniques related to recruiting. Several institutions have worked hard on changing the image it wishes to project to the public. This change has not been without associated costs, which can range from the purchasing of expensive stationery, first-class brochures and publications, to media blitzes. This has added further strain on limited financial resources because money has been diverted to these endeavors in an attempt to cope. As a function of declining enrollment following decades of unprecedented growth, universities have been scrambling to make do with constrained financial resources.

BACKGROUND

The total enrollment in institutions of higher education in 1957 was 3.3 million. By 1960 there were 2,000 institutions with 3.6 million students. The 18-year-old population in that year was 3.6 million. In 1967, student population had grown to 6.4 million. During this 10-year time span higher education came close to doubling. To accommodate such growth the number of institutions increased to 2,573 by 1970. By 1977, student enrollment had grown to 11.3 million and by 1980 the number of institutions had expanded to 3,150. However, only 4.2 million 18-year-olds existed for these institutions, and the number declined as baby boomers moved on (Merante, 1987).

During this boom period the availability of federal funds increased at an amazing rate — $648 million in 1960, $2.5 billion in 1970, and $7.8 billion in 1980. Student growth slowed in the 1980s, but the increase continued with another 1.2 million more students enrolled in institutions of higher education by 1987 compared to 1977. In only three decades (1957–87) enrollment increased almost fourfold: 3.3 to 12.5 million. Private institution enrollment doubled (1.4 to 2.8 million), while enrollment in public institutions took an almost five-fold leap, from about 2 million to 10 million students. When one analyzes what happened to the higher education system during this period, it is easy to understand why financial woes were jut around the corner. It is incredible the system has not broken down (Halloran, 1989).

The rapid enrollment expansion of the 1960s caused college administrators to focus planning efforts on space and finances. The thrust was to expand. Even campuses with stable enrollments added new and improved facilities such as libraries, computer centers, and science laboratories. Old buildings were not removed, only renovated, when new ones were added, and investments in plants rose sharply.

A steady stream of qualified students seemed constantly available for institutions. Growth was taken for granted. Facilities were constructed to instruct the growing student pool, and new and innovative degree programs were added to institutional offerings to provide a competitive edge in attracting the expanded student population (Morrell, 1986).

State governments were pressured to provide funds to higher education because this nation was becoming a knowledge-driven economy. A college education was seen as essential if a person was to advance in society. Getting a college degree had become as important to today's youth as a high school education was to the youth of previous decades.

All of the positive dimensions associated with higher education growth created little demand for systematic or efficient allocation of resources. Little thought was given to where funds would come from. Thought focused on how to continue to expand. College and university leaders paid little attention to developing a planning process, particularly with regard to managing insufficient resources. Even with continued growth in enrollment, however, the first concerns were raised in the 1970s.

Sharply rising inflation figures, coupled with the burden of providing for the operation and maintenance of new construction from the 1960s, forced institutional leaders to raise tuition, seek additional external funds, and, in state-supported universities, approach the legislature for increased funding to maintain operating costs. Growth and the concomitant needs it produces almost always left institutions behind the monetary eight ball; prospects continued to look good for meeting needs if only an institution could make it through to another year. However, from an administrative perspective, things started to change in the wrong direction.

By the late 1970s the number of high school graduates had peaked and their numbers declined in the 1980s. This reduction increased competition among the universities. New strategies were formulated for attracting quality students. Some institutions leading this charge revised their admission requirements by making them more stringent, hoping to project an image that a degree earned at that institution was of greater value on the open market. This approach was, in most cases, highly successful. A fallout from this procedure was an increase in the number and quality of student applications to the institutions employing this approach. Institutional profiles then indicated how scores on standardized exams had increased for the incoming freshman class. A media game developed whereby institutions would seek to be on the list of "best buys" based on the student body profile of high ACT/SAT scores, admission requirements, faculty, and cost. Whether the list reflected reality is a question to be addressed elsewhere; it was important to chief executives to not only make the list, but also to be as high up as possible because of its impact on recruiting and freshman applications.

During this same period, particularly in the 1980s, educational funding declined. Legislatures were no longer willing to foot the bill. Quality came under close scrutiny. The expansion of the 1960s and 1970s and the related decline in standards led to several critical reports concerning the academy. In the public sector, demand to hold institutions accountable has led to the current wave of assessment evaluations that have become a dominant theme of accrediting agencies. This new thrust has added to a university's operating costs, in some cases $1 million or more. Higher education has learned that accountability is not cheap. Private institutions have also come under increasing pressure to assess the quality of their programs and students with each passing year.

The swollen population of institutions has moved from an era of unprecedented and unplanned growth to an era of retrenchment, budgetary cutbacks, accountability, and reallocation of resources. Officials of public and private universities must do more with less and are faced with an unfavorable economic climate in the 1990s. The result of this dramatic shift is an imbalance between resources and demand. The associated issues facing higher education in the 1990s require new strategies for problem solving that will include behavior and attitude change among the participants.

CHALLENGE OF MANAGING
DECLINING RESOURCES

Managing institutions with declining revenues is extremely complex. One of the main sources for reduced budgets lies in declining federal and state support, with particularly significant cutbacks and shifts occurring in federal student assistance programs. Many institutions address the loss of federal and state assistance with increased tuition for students, but this problem only becomes a vicious cycle as financial aid decreases.

Obviously, since sufficient funding increases are not likely, officials must develop alternatives and plans in order to cope. Higher education leaders will probably learn and borrow ideas from business leaders forced to cope with stiff foreign competition in the 1970s and 1980s. How well these ideas will work is yet to be determined. Careful university planning, coupled with innovation and faculty cooperation, will be keys to success in the 1990s.

The issues and challenges associated with declining revenues cannot be easily separated and dealt with in a singular vein, as they are intertwined and affect each other in a complex fashion. However, for discussion purposes the issues will be identified and potential strategies for coping will follow at the end of the text.

Student Recruitment

A declining college-age student population during the 1980s increased competition for students. Particular emphasis was on recruiting the best students. As institutions today compete for students, a natural inclination is to increase dollars available for scholarship funds. Increased funding for scholarships, during a time when funds are insufficient to meet all needs, means shifting funds from other sources. The funds to be reallocated for scholarships is an important question. One approach to helping alleviate this problem has been to solicit funds through annual alumni drives, special events, and telephone solicitations. Universities have also made scholarships one of their top priorities during major fundraising campaigns. Universities have been successful with this approach because individuals generally are willing to support students with scholarship funds. Increased competition for students also requires that the best-qualified faculty be obtained by the institution for instruction.

Faculty Recruitment

The need to employ the best faculty mandates that funds be available for competitive faculty salaries and necessary faculty perks, such as equipment, professional travel, and research support. With a steady or declining revenue base, where will these funds be obtained?

The problems associated with hiring new faculty at highly competitive salaries is that an imbalance of salaries across divisions and among faculty within a departmental division is created. This is fine if the rachet principle can be invoked, that is, the salaries of faculty who have served the university with distinction for many years are raised to the levels of the new hirings. Salary adjustments should occur every year if the process is to be equitable. What institution could afford to operate under such guidelines? Even greater pressure today is being exerted in the favor of new faculty because of perceived or actual shortages within an academic field, exacerbating the problem of salary compression.

Today, the competition to hire qualified faculty is further intensified by the threat of impending shortages of doctoral graduates. Recent data compiled by the Association of American

Universities (AAU) in a report entitled "The Ph.D. Shortage: The Federal Role" indicates intensified competition as demand for Ph.D.s exceeds the supply (Staff, 1990). This shortage, already most evident in disciplines such as business, is spreading to other academic areas (nursing, computer science, engineering, and mathematics, just to mention a few) and creates significant employment questions and issues for higher education officials.

How long can universities avoid drawing a line on salary demands of prospective faculty while maintaining a viable and productive scholarly faculty? Will officials and faculty be forced to hire non-Ph.D.s in roles normally reserved for terminally degree-prepared persons, and what impact will this have on matters such as tenure and promotion guidelines and decisions? Can universities maintain accepted standards and norms for employment and tenure in this time of dwindling availability of doctorates and increased competition for employment? How academic leaders are able to cope with this matter will have a tremendous impact on the financial and personnel policies of the institution.

One potential solution to the challenge of a faculty shortage undertaken by some universities is to "grow their own" faculty. These faculty members may occupy a non-tenure-track position of instructor. The institution encourages the faculty member to develop a degree plan to earn a terminal degree and helps support the faculty member through a leave of absence with pay, summer sabbatical, or some other creative idea. Once the degree is near completion the individual's position is changed to the tenure-track slot with a promotion to assistant professor.

Another innovative approach is to support financially the best undergraduates in their quest to earn an advanced degree. The individual commits to return after the degree is completed. A variation of this theme has been applied by several states in helping minorities earn their terminal degree through these state scholarships, obligating these individuals to come back to the state and teach in the higher education system.

Accreditation

Another challenge requiring increased attention and funding is accreditation. Achieving accreditation is a distinctive facet of higher education programs. The status of accreditation plays a significant role in the recruiting of students and faculty to a university. Revised accreditation guidelines of groups such as the American Assembly of Collegiate Schools of Business (AACSB) and National Council for the Accreditation of Teacher Education (NCATE) have placed a tremendous burden on already diminished university resources.

Accreditation mandates concerning reduced teaching loads, scholarship, library holdings, course offerings, and enrollment caps require the commitment of additional resources for that college or school to be successful.

University administrators are also confronted with the problem of where to obtain the necessary funds for the accreditation process, which usually results in another university effort being cut, or receiving diminished support for at least a year, if not longer. A corollary problem with accreditation, especially professional school accreditation, is the negative impact on faculties in the arts and sciences. They may not have accreditation leverage and therefore may not receive reduced teaching loads, support for scholarship, library resources, smaller class sizes, and so forth. The imbalance is then one of finances and morale, which can undermine the collegial atmosphere so highly prized on a university campus.

Acquisition and Maintenance of Equipment and Facilities

The competitive posture necessary for faculty and student recruitment and university viability mandates state-of-the-art equipment for instruction and research. The latest laboratory equipment and first-rate facilities are viewed as necessary for being on the cutting edge of knowledge. These factors are viewed as absolutely essential to a university's success. Even in institutions whose primary mission is teaching, equipment and facilities are a major concern. Yet, the costs for such items are spiraling upward at an unprecedented rate (typically at rates much higher than inflation), and college and university budgets cannot keep pace.

Equally important to the teaching and research efforts of a university are library resources and holdings. The subscription rates to journals are escalating at a frightening rate, with some increasing in cost by 200 percent to 300 percent since 1980.

In addition there are costs for maintenance, storage, and security. Faculties avidly stress the need for these purchases as probably second in importance to their salaries. Can universities afford these costs for all programs, or will decisions of priority have to be made that may eliminate certain programs?

Faculty will move from one institution to another if the building or laboratory space is deemed inadequate, especially if they are in a discipline that affords them mobility. The building explosion that occurred in the mid-to-late 1960s and early 1970s is now creating one of the largest dilemmas confronting higher education officials. The libraries, dormitories, and classroom buildings built when enrollments were booming and growth seemed unlimited now present tremendous drains on limited resources because an aging plant must be maintained.

The National Association of College and University Business Officers has stated that $70 billion in repairs and replacements are needed on college campuses, with $20.5 billion classified as urgent (Grassmuck, 1990). As university officials built and expanded physical plants, little, if any, planning was done to accommodate the maintenance needs of these buildings. Long-term budgeting for maintenance was nonexistent; as buildings aged and funds dwindled, the adage of "if it ain't broke, don't fix it" prevailed. Unfortunately, that philosophy does not work, because even "if it ain't broke," it still needs maintenance.

The philosophy of deferred maintenance has created a vast drain on already stretched resources. Deteriorating facilities also have a detrimental effect on recruiting top-quality students and faculty. The image of the university is visible to a prospective student and faculty member immediately upon inspection of the physical plant. Competition for students and faculty mandates an adequate and even attractive physical plant. Faculty need safe and adequate facilities to conduct research and teach, and students demand the same. Laboratory space and functional equipment can often be the difference in retaining or recruiting a faculty member to a particular academic program.

The issue of facilities and associated costs has only been magnified by federal and state legislation in areas such as environmental compliance and handicapped access to buildings. Asbestos and hazardous materials have caused administrators nightmares. University leaders must determine ways to meet the costs of physical plant maintenance and alteration, as well as hazardous waste disposal. Environmental issues have simply added to the dilemma of maintenance upkeep. Where will these funds come from within already strained budgets?

The physical expansion of the university plant has produced ever-increasing utility and insurance costs, which have risen faster than the inflation rate. Even though decisions can be made regarding what to insure and for how much, some form of insurance must be maintained that always seems to spiral upward. Universities have taken great pains through efficiency measures to implement reductions in the utility costs of educating faculty and staff, but the dollar figure continues to escalate. Utility costs in particular must be paid and cannot be deferred, as can routine maintenance. Without an increase in budget funds to offset such costs, utilities can create a substantial drain on a university's budget. The costs must be addressed and, therefore, academic instruction funds are often shifted or not provided in order to offset utility increases.

Rising Health Costs

Rising health costs present another almost uncontrollable drain on dwindling resources. Health care now represents millions of dollars in a university's operating funds. The increases in health care programs can often constitute a double drain on limited resources. Most universities either match employee contributions to health care or pay the entire cost. In matching costs, the double drain results from the university having to increase its contribution and at the same time deal with faculty demands for pay increases to offset the individual rising costs of health insurance. In the ever-increasing competition for faculty, the health care options available to a prospective faculty member can be as important in deciding whether to accept or reject an offer as is salary and other research support available from the university. Excessive pressure is created for administrators to solve these problems and make everyone happy. Can administrators be Pied Pipers?

Program Maintenance and Enhancement

University leaders will need to maintain programs in which they can excel. Selective investment (Grassmuck, 1990) will be necessary and unavoidable. Decisions concerning the programs to be maintained or enhanced must incorporate information about the programs that best serve regional or state needs, and information provided by an "environmental scanning committee" will become an important working component of university operations. Determining who will fit in the membership of such a committee will be of primary importance to the functional success of the university. While universities are making decisions about what programs to maintain, decisions must also be made about program expansion.

To help in this quest of making good decisions, a growing number of institutions have created a university committee that functions as a think tank. Often called a university planning committee, this group of individuals functions outside the normal governance structure of the university. The group is comprised of faculty, administrators, staff, students, and members of the governing board. Its role is to advise the president on any and all challenges and issues facing the institution. This group is just as likely to play a passive or active role in helping to initiate or support innovation. The committee addresses a host of topics that includes, but is not limited to, evaluating programs (new or old), resources, goals, missions, university image, recruitment and retention strategies, admission policies, technology, and so forth. This group helps to insure that the university has a game plan that is followed when attempting to make the wisest choices and decisions in all facets of university functioning. In the 1990s chief executive officers will seek the advice and counsel of such groups in order to be successful.

Faculty Salaries

No discussion of issues of the 1990s would be complete without the topic of faculty salaries. Salaries and additional benefits have been touched upon in previous notes, but the issue is burdensome enough to warrant additional discussion. Diminishing numbers of Ph.D. faculty, plus the need to have the best faculty available in order to maintain quality programs and recruit the best students, all add up to monumental problems for higher education.

Colleges must offer higher salaries to keep faculty in high-demand fields and to attract persons from those fields. Several problems from the demand to pay higher salaries will confront university leaders. New assistant professors may demand and get higher starting salaries than associate or full professors at the institution. This will create morale problems, especially among faculty who have maintained a commitment to an institution and stayed with the program over the long haul. It will appear to individuals who have been at the institution a significant number of years that they are not as prized as new, inexperienced faculty, and this feeling will make it extremely difficult to create a sense of community among colleagues. Administrators must create a balance between old and new while being market competitive.

A partial solution would be to set aside salary enhancement funds for the most productive or valuable faculty members. Administrators should try to stem the tide of having valuable faculty seek employment elsewhere by demonstrating appreciation in a tangible way. Once a search for a new position is initiated, the probability of the faculty member leaving in the near future increases. Proactive approaches to resolving this challenge are crucial if the institution is to retain the best members of a dedicated faculty.

ATTEMPTS TO COPE

Declining resources and increasing costs present particular challenges for higher education administrators and faculty because they are not prepared to deal with these issues. Basically, the problem is one of financial management, and the vast majority of higher education personnel are not adequately prepared to resolve these difficult administrative decision-making issues (Levine, 1978). A primary reason for this situation is that faculty search committees look for individuals who are academicians. Emphasis is placed on an individual's scholarship, grantsmanship, teaching expertise, collegiality, and so forth when seeking to hire a dean, vice president of academic affairs, or president of an institution. Leadership ability holds much greater weight in the selection process than management skills or financial knowledge when filling these important administrative posts.

A lack of knowledge concerning the budgeting process often leaves the chief academic and executive officer at the mercy of the individuals who are in charge of financial management, typically, the vice president of administrative affairs (or some similar title). Faculties have great fears about decisions being made by financial officers concerning the allocation of university resources.

Anxiety can reach a fever pitch when a faculty feels it has no input about how resources are distributed. All too often the faculty perceives that the financial affairs side of the house is not being as forthright with information as it should be. Compounding this concern is the perception by the faculty that individuals overseeing the distribution of funds do not wish to share budget and revenue data. This approach usually raises a red flag to the faculty. Speculation about where the money is being spent abound, and a major concern arises that the support areas of the institution are receiving a larger slice of the pie than is appropriate. In those institutions where faculties do have input, there is the concomitant danger that having a voice in the process and exerting control over how the dollars should be budgeted often get intermingled.

Who should control these scarce resources? Who are the individuals involved in decisions related to potential cuts? Has there been dialogue about eliminating degree programs or faculty slots? Each of these topics evokes tremendous stress, anxiety, and conflict within an institution (Levine, 1979).

The psychological trauma produced by these questions, if the faculty is not given adequate input, tends to reduce effective and cooperative problem solving — the exact strategy needed in times of reduced revenues and retrenchment. That most universities function in a slow, deliberate, and decentralized decision-making process also makes management and decision making related to retrenchment especially difficult. Growth in the 1960s, 1970s, and early 1980s, with ready availability of funds and students, did not provide a basis for systematic or efficient allocation of resources. Hindsight is said to produce the best sight; and it is, therefore, easy to now say that a Golden Rule for planning is to plan for exigencies and cutbacks when times are good.

Planning for Retrenchment

By assuming a planning posture for what happens if a university loses certain resources, an institution is better able to deal with alternative strategies for reduction in a period when stress, conflict, and anxiety are at their lowest. Hypothetical scenarios can be built upon sound professional judgment, and people will be more open in their planning when discussing potential changes versus real changes. Also, planning for retrenchment during periods of prosperity fits well into the higher education framework because of the slow, deliberate, and decentralized decision process. The important role of all constituents in the decision process can be maintained, thereby eliminating faculty concerns about administrators making unilateral decisions, or, worse yet, decisions being dictated by the finance office on a profit-loss basis. Trust and openness is maintained and evident for all members of the university community to see. Unfortunately, the Golden Rule of retrenchment planning in good times did not occur, so strategies and alternatives must be employed now to cope with the immediate realities of decline or insufficient funding.

Cuts, retrenchment, and redistribution of resources create persons and interest groups on campus seeking to protect their turf. Anxiety, conflict, and stress are common reactions; alternatively, some groups or individuals see a window of opportunity and attempt to better their positions by getting the ear of decision makers at the expense of others (Mintzberg, 1983; Pettigrew, 1973). Campus leaders involved in determining process and policy must be aware of the fear-of-loss groups and the opportunity-to-gain groups as cuts or redistribution of resources issues are dealt with on campus. Caution must be taken not to grease the squeaky wheel. A balance of the needs of all parties must be maintained while actively involving all components of the university in the decision-making process.

Involving All Components

This is where the role of an environmental scanning or planning committee can be important in helping to set appropriate priorities. Campus leaders who understand the big picture of how a university functions should be selected for these committees.

A model of collegial (participative), representative decision making is used in making cuts or retrenchment decisions. The dilemma is that the collegial model can be cumbersome and slow, and decisions may need to be active and swift. What then are the ingredients of an effective coping strategy that is collegial but swift? The private and business sectors, faced with the same issues of decline and competition, drastically reduce costs or overhead while increasing productivity.

Universities can incorporate certain principles from the private sector, but they must be tempered with the deliberate decision-making style of universities. Private enterprise employs a top-down management style, often with minimal input from employees (faculty, in the case of universities), that can create swift, immediate change. Universities cannot completely copy that style, but they certainly can emulate certain principles with modification to the university environment.

Strategic Planning

Strategic planning is one aspect of the business world that can be duplicated on the university campus. The corporate world has engaged in strategic planning for years, but colleges and universities have paid little attention to this concept (Morrell, 1986). Universities primarily have had an internal focus orientation to growth of activities within the institution, predicated on a willingness of students and government to provide the funds to support expansion of activities. Strategic planning for business is driven by competition in the private sector and the need to plan wisely, allocating resources in the best interest of the company. Strategic planning can be viewed as the survival of an organization and its attempt to realize its goals, strengths, and the wise use of resources (Morrell, 1986).

Since available funds significantly affect any planning activities, both expansion and reduction, the budgeting process is at the heart of strategic planning. A budget merely indicates the priorities and mission of the institution and reflects the manner in which the institution will allocate resources and plan to accomplish goals within an academic year (Meisinger & Dubeck, 1984). Universities must move to a strategic planning model, focusing on budgeting for goals and objectives.

The strategic planning process should be both immediate, dealing with cuts and reallocation of resources, and long-term. Central to the issue of strategic planning is the question of who participates and in what manner. Obviously, several members of the university community need active involvement, but academic deans and department chairs are crucial to the effort. The academic leadership of the university resides among these groups, and the academic programs are at the heart of the university's very existence. Faculty leaders and key financial personnel must also be involved in the process.

As already mentioned, a key component to effective strategic planning is the composition of the planning committee. The president and vice presidents are always participants, along with the academic deans. Department chairs must also be intimately involved, but the size of the university will dictate some form of selective participation from this group. It is probably best to allow the chairs input, via a selection mechanism of their representatives to a planning group. Faculty involvement is key to the success of the planning committee.

The faculty participants' profiles must be given serious consideration when selected for involvement. A balance of perspectives from the faculty is paramount to viable input; therefore, faculty must represent several dimensions. Senior faculty members with long tenures must be included, but faculty with a vision of the university's future must also be selected. It is also very important that the faculty membership assure continuity in membership from year to year, as planning should not be viewed as a one-time process. Obviously, the faculty composition will be such as to reflect a distribution among the disciplines of the campus.

The staff should also be intimately involved in this process. Staff members can significantly influence how students perceive the institution. The impact of these individuals is felt in every facet of university functioning — recruitment, registration, housing, financial aid, academic and administrative offices, and so forth.

The last constituency that needs to be included is the governing board. Including a member from the board is crucial if the board is to understand the goals of the university and be as committed to achieving those goals as the faculty, staff, and administration. It also helps bring into focus the challenges the university faces. This information can then be transmitted to other board members to help the institution reach its full potential.

Every institution has its own character because of its history, mission, size, location, type of support, and faculty composition (Meisinger & Dubeck, 1984). These dimensions will determine the way in which participants will interact in the planning and budgeting process. Strategic planning with the right combination of individuals will incorporate all the best aspects of collegial governance into the budgeting process. The initial task of such a committee should be to re-examine the institution's mission. By focusing on that mission, future decisions about allocation of funds have a central point for discussion.

Budget Considerations

The deliberations of the planning committee must be incorporated into budgeting decisions. The budget committee should be a smaller group of individuals, but one that retains all important segments of the university community. Faculty who serve on this committee should have a minimum term of three to five years, and a rotation system should be developed where budgeting expertise is continually maintained. Several institutions have developed a system whereby the president and vice president of the faculty senate serve as the main faculty voice. A host of problems exists with the employment of this process, as a faculty member typically gets to serve, in almost all instance, a maximum of two years on the budget committee.

The main focus of the budget committee should be to carry out the institution's mission, given the available resources. The president and vice president of the faculty senate usually represent the most important political constituency on campus. Can decisions be made pertaining to the best use of financial resources when faculty members will be looking to see if their political representatives have sold out? Can the institution afford to have individuals representing the faculty senate who yell the loudest and therefore grab the lion's share of the funds? In either case the university is the potential loser. A related problem is whether or not the best faculty representatives, with vision and concern for the institution's growth and development, are giving valuable input.

A group that gives important information to both the planning and budgeting committees is the environmental scanning committee. This is a recent phenomenon within the academy, gaining in status and importance over the last decade. This committee's focus is to evaluate local, regional, and state needs during the next five to ten years. Input is sought from a variety of resources, for example: local and state governments, elementary and secondary schools, health organizations, the business community, and chambers of commerce. The information obtained seeks to evaluate the institution's reputation, how well its graduates are doing, the visibility of the university, and, most important of all, the perceived needs and trends of the region over the next decade. The committee's task is to assess how many of these perceived needs and trends fit the institution's mission and to send this information to both the planning and budget committees for action, if deemed appropriate.

Difficult and potentially unpopular decisions will have to be made. Every potential solution and innovation to make the institution as lean as possible without affecting academic quality should be pursued. One area that may be able to stand trimming, given the tremendous growth in the 1960s, 1970s, and early 1980s, is support personnel.

Reducing Support Personnel (Streamlining)

There has been a definite growth in the number of positions carrying the title assistant or associate that has spread into the vice president's office, dean's office, registrar's office, and so forth. A good percentage of this occurred as administrators retired or advanced to other positions. The functions performed by one person were often subdivided among several individuals. Many jokes were told on campus concerning the worth of the individual who had just left, or the value of the replacements.

The staff expansion was partly to reduce the heavy work load the previous individual had undertaken, and partly to adjust to the increasing student population and the desire to be more responsive in a number of areas previously overlooked. On example was the desire to be more sensitive to student needs in counseling and remediation. The time may be right, as was recently pointed out by Zemsky and Massy (1990) in the *Chronicle of Higher Education,* for staffs to be reduced and for faculty to share greater responsibility for delivering services to students. Savings could then be redistributed to other, more crucial areas of the institution.

A common complaint among the faculty is that administrative and staff personnel are top heavy. This appears to be a universal complaint, no matter what campus you are on. Time and energy need to be directed to addressing the question of how institutions can streamline their functioning so that resources can be diverted to the most crucial needs of the institution. Commitment and understanding must exist at all levels of the university for there to be a successful solution.

Communication

Understanding via communication is possibly the most important challenge facing administrators in attempting to deal with the fiscal realities of the 1990s. It is imperative that the faculty knows the plans and directions of the university. They must be an integral part of those plans and directions. It is important that they feel as much ownership as the president, vice president, dean, or department chair. This is equal in importance to the commitment that all segments of the university make to the mission of the university if the institution is to have a chance to grow and prosper. The difficulty of establishing strong communication links should not be underestimated. All members of the university community should feel they have had or will have significant input into the mission and goal statements. The need to be kept abreast of how fiscal resources will be used to meet these stated goals and objectives is paramount. All individuals need to feel that the decision-making process and communication flow in both directions.

CONCLUSION

A final word of caution: chief academic and executive officers who attempt to shoulder the burden of constrained resources without involving the university community will be in for a rude awakening. The faculty either will be alienated and feel helpless, leading to extreme morale problems, or it will organize to put pressure on changing budget priorities by threatening votes of confidence.

One unacceptable but often used means of resolving the issue of declining resources is an across-the-board cut, which appears to be an easy and acceptable means of managing reductions (Hardy, 1984). The belief is that all parties share equally in the loss of revenues and that across-the-board hiring and pay freezes treat everyone in an equitable manner. This approach is fallacious and will often reward inefficient, ineffective units while penalizing the more effective and productive components of the university.

Across-the-board cuts are certainly the easiest to implement, because they initially give the impression of fairness. This process of reduction may appear to work for initial cuts, but eventually the process is doomed to failure because the university's reduction or redirection efforts are completed by default. Across-the-board cuts do not establish priorities or foster the mission of the institution but merely distribute the pain and frustration across the campus. Since across-the-board cuts are usually made from the top and filter down, they will eventually, if maintained as the operating philosophy for coping, doom the administration to failure. Across-the-board cuts violate the collegial model because little, if any, input is sought or needed by the administration from key academic leaders and the faculty about the priorities of the institution and how their programs fit into those priorities. Since across-the-board cuts are centralized decisions about reductions, these cuts are viewed with great disdain by the faculty and impede its involvement in problem solving. Furthermore, if strategic planning is a part of the university's model of operating, there will be no need for across-the-board cuts.

Another chapter could be written addressing the war stories that have been told because of top-down decisions. Ultimately, university administrators must realize that faculty can be productive or unproductive in fostering the institution's mission, depending on their perceived voice and level of involvement.

In summary, the university's administrative team faces many challenges and opportunities for creative solutions when attempting to satisfy all members of the academic community on such topics as university funding, mission, and institutional governance during the 1990s. The issues created in the 1960s, 1970s, and 1980s relating to growth and expansion will force a new breed of leadership to develop. These individuals must have more than mere leadership abilities, they must be versed in the budgetary process and in how to employ the kind of strategic and long-range planning into the everyday functioning of the institution that will result in a clear commitment to the university's mission. The decisions that must be made will be enhanced by information gained from the environmental scanning committee. Challenges have always brought out the best of individuals within the academy. Universities can look forward to bold new leaders and the resultant innovation these individuals will bring to higher education well into the 21st century.

REFERENCES

Grassmuck, K. (1990, January 31). Clouded economy prompts colleges to weigh changes. *Chronicle of Higher Education, 39,* A1, A28, A30.

Halloran, W. F. (1989). Is there life in deaning? Conversations in the arts and sciences. *Council of Colleges of Arts and Sciences Newsletter, 10*(6), 2.

Hardy, C. (1984). The management of university cutbacks: Politics, planning and participation. *Canadian Journal of Higher Education, 14*(1), 59–69.

Levine, C. (1979). More on cutback management: Hard questions for hard times. *Public Administration Review, 39*(2), 179–83.

Levine, C. (1978). Organizational decline and cutback management. *Public Administration Review, 38*(4), 316–25.

Meisinger, R., & Dubeck, L. (1984). The faculty role in budgeting. *Business Officer, 17*(10), 17–21.

Merante, J. (1987). Organizing to manage enrollment. *College Board Review, 140,* 20–23.

Mintzberg, H. (1983). *Power in and around organizations.* Englewood Cliffs, NJ: Prentice-Hall.

Morrell, L. (1986). Strategic planning for colleges and universities. *College Board Review, 140,* 20–23.

Pettigrew, A. M. (1973). *The politics of organizational decision making.* London: Tavistock.

Staff. (1990, January 29). The Ph.D. shortage: The federal role. *Higher Education & National Affairs, 39,* 2.

Zemsky, R., & Massy, W. F. (1990). Cost containment: Committing to a new economic reality. *Change, 22,* 16–23.

4

Developing a Campus Climate
for Diversity in the 21st Century

Roberto P. Haro

America is moving backward — not forward — in
its efforts to achieve the full participation of minority
citizens in the life and prosperity of the nation.

In education, employment, income, health, lon-
gevity, and other basic measures of individual and
social well-being, gaps persist — and in some cases
are widening — between members of minority
groups and the majority population.

If we allow these disparities to continue, the United
States inevitably will suffer a compromised quality
of life and a lower standard of living. Social conflict
will intensify. Our ability to compete in world
markets will decline, our domestic economy will
falter, our national security will be endangered. In
brief, we will find ourselves unable to fulfill the
promise of the American dream.

— American Council on Education and
Education Commission of the States, 1988

The report of the Commission on Minority Participation in Education
and American Life, a joint effort by the American Council on
Education and the Education Commission of the States entitled *One-
Third of a Nation* (1988), contains sobering information about the
changing demographics in the United States and the challenges a
rapidly increasing minority population presents for our society.
Educational groups, especially those concerned with colleges and
universities, are searching for alternatives to address the low
representation and limited status of minorities in institutions of
higher education. Some campuses are experimenting with programs

and activities to recruit and retain underrepresented groups, especially those from lower socioeconomic groups. Others seem uncertain about what to do and where to begin. Some far-sighted groups, however, are beginning to forge a new agenda that will prepare U.S. youth for the 21st century (Turning Points, 1989 National Task Force for Minority Achievement in Higher Education, 1990).

Most educators and higher educational policymakers are aware of the rapid increases of minorities in the college-age cohort (Levine & Associates, 1989). The report on high school graduates prepared by the Western Interstate Commission on Higher Education (WICHE) provides a graphic set of projections for the immediate future (WICHE, 1988). There will be more pronounced changes in some regions than in others where varying economic conditions and growth in minority populations occur. The WICHE report on population changes and the future of the Southwest is a compelling document that focuses on educational needs (WICHE, 1987). However, some institutions have responded to this challenge with efforts that are not well thought out (Haro, 1991). Many major publicly supported institutions have aggressive campaigns to recruit increased numbers of minorities to their campuses (Task Force on Black Student Eligibility, 1990). But little thought has been given to what effects an increased minority presence may have on our campuses (*Harvard Educational Review,* 1988). As institutions try to diversify two issues are paramount: improving access to higher education for minorities and determining the effects an increased minority presence may have on our institutions. These two key issues are intertwined.

The Numbers Game and the Revolving Door Syndrome

Some institutions have a narrow perspective on achieving diversity. For many, it is simply a matter of recruiting more underrepresented minorities. There is a visible scramble among elite and prestigious colleges for well-prepared minority students, but they are reluctant to admit any at-risk minority students. At some publicly supported institutions, particularly in the western United States, legislative language may be in place calling for the increased representation of minorities and the economically and educationally disadvantaged on campus (Education Commission of the States, 1986). Public colleges and universities that feel compelled, for whatever reason, to increase the number of underrepresented students may adopt a target strategy, that is, they aggressively recruit minorities to maintain a desired enrollment level. However, if the campus climate is not hospitable to these students, many of them drop out after a year or more (Clewell & Ficklen, 1986). We have learned that many underrepresented students leave for nonacademic reasons (Rendon & Amaury, 1987/88). The aggressive recruitment and high drop out rate of these students is often referred to as the revolving door syndrome. How can an institution improve access and retention, and graduate an increased number of underrepresented students?

Campus Climate

We cannot expect new types of students to adapt easily to a campus designed for another clientele. Such campuses are not well prepared to cope with these new students. Moreover, each campus has a unique culture that reflects to some degree the values and accepted practices of the local or regional society (Kuh & Whitt, 1988). While there are some constants within the academy, such as the role of the faculty and the educational and research mission of the institution, norms, and standards that affect attitudes and condition behavior, our prevalent college culture has deep roots directly traceable to Europe and England. Along the Atlantic Seaboard colleges and universities, especially the older, private ones, celebrate these English and European traditions (Bloom, 1987). African-Americans, Asian-Americans, Hispanics, and Native Americans were, for the most part, never involved in the development of these institutions and are, therefore, like "strangers from different shores" (Takaki, 1989). When minorities arrive on campus as new students, new staff persons, or as newly appointed faculty members, norms and traditions may be troublesome to them. Minorities learn to accommodate in order to survive. This does not mean, however, that we are pleased by the dominant cultural manifestations on a campus that relegate us to subculture roles and marginalize us (Beckham, 1987/88). Even if we do adopt the outward manifestations of the dominant culture on campus, what price will we pay, and can we ever be certain of acceptance? The article by Reyes and Halcon provides an important insight on how racism continues to operate in academia and works against minorities (1988).

Leaders in education must adopt a new commitment to make the transition from numerical diversity to interactive pluralism. It begins at the K–12 levels, where a new vision must be defined for schools as a place where all ethnic and racial groups can appreciate their differences in a process of mutual enrichment (University Committee on Minority Issues, 1989). At the college level new ways must be identified for minorities and those from the larger society to acknowledge and build mutual respect for similarities as well as differences. The following strategies should be considered.

Set Priorities

The president and top executives must publicly announce their goal for eliminating racial and ethnic disparities on campus and state their firm commitment to educational equity (American Council on Education, 1989). Leaders within the faculty, staff, and student body must join with the president and senior executives to craft a program that will achieve educational equity. There are several models available. For the small liberal arts college, the work of the President's Task Force on Minority Presence at Saint Mary's College of California is exemplary (Report of the President's Task Force on Minority Presence, 1989). For a larger private university, the *Final Report of the University Committee on Minority Issues* (University Committee on Minority Issues, 1989) at Stanford University is an important document. Finally, for a publicly supported university, the *Madison Plan* (1988) at the University of Wisconsin, Madison, offers much food for thought.

Crafting a plan for diversity, however, is not enough. The president must make the implementation of a diversity plan a key priority and back it up with needed resources and continuing commitment. Moreover, strategies must be devised to track and evaluate progress toward campus diversity regularly. A public self-assessment is required to determine successes and identify areas that may require attention. Unless the president is completely committed to carrying out a plan for diversity, needed change will be more promise than practice. The implementation of a successful educational equity program at San Jose State University reflects continuing administrative support (Rodriquez, 1989).

Provide Comprehensive and Integrated Support Services

The institution must develop support services that closely link academic and student activities. Programs that bridge the social and educational gaps minorities face are essential (Minority Recruitment/Retention Task Force, 1989). Specialized minority enclaves that tend to marginalize these students must be phased out in favor of programs and activities that interface all students. This should include extended classes covering required materials, tutoring, learning laboratories, collaborative study groups, and active counseling that pulls students in the direction of a major. Majority and minority students should be encouraged to mentor each other, study together, learn from each other, depend upon each other, and socialize with each other. An important model is the Counseling and Academic Skills Development (CASD) Program at Pennsylvania State University, which provides individualized counseling and academic support services for minority undergraduates (American Council on Education, 1989).

Establish a Nonthreatening Social Environment

The campus climate and infrastructure must be examined carefully to determine how the dominant culture is manifested. Two critical areas for review are the academic structure and programs, and the out-of-class and social experiences encountered by students (Odell & Mock, 1989). Academic programs and staff services must be reviewed thoroughly to identify any attitudes and practices that are biased or culturally discriminatory. Staff in support services, like admissions and financial aid, must begin to understand how students from different cultural backgrounds perceive them (Jones, Terrell, & Duggar, 1991). This review and change process must include everyone connected with the institution: faculty, staff, students, and especially trustees and alumni. Social machinery such as fraternities and sororities or social clubs must begin to incorporate different cultural attitudes and expectations and eliminate biases that rank one type of student over others. The Madison Plan at the University of Wisconsin contains several initiatives to improve campus climate for minorities (*Madison Plan,* 1988).

A key strategy to improve campus climate for minorities and other underrepresented groups involves the development of a campuswide commission that includes representatives from senior faculty, staff and student leaders, alumni, a trustee or two, and two or more community leaders in the immediate area. Reporting directly to the president, this group should review all aspects of the campus for discriminatory conditions and assist with the development of strategies and activities to overcome racially biased attitudes and behavior. Such a commission should be long lived, and its leadership must meet regularly with the president and the president's chief advisors.

Stress Quality

The issue of high standards has traditionally cast minorities as at risk and deficient, particularly at some prestigious institutions. However, educational quality is often used as a double-edged sword. Selective institutions have in the past excluded minorities disproportionately: some because they do not meet high standards, others because they are perceived as overachievers. Diversity and excellence are possible, but without diversity excellence is not possible.

Several programs have demonstrated how successful minorities can be at highly selective institutions. Brooklyn College provides a first-class education. One-third of its student body is African-American and Hispanic, and it graduates students proportionately. The Mathematics Workshop Program affiliated with the Professional Development Program at the University of California at Berkeley is the brainchild of Uri Treisman. It is a highly successful program that should serve as a model for other institutions. It is critical for minority students to escape any stigma that casts them as second-class or inferior students. If minorities are motivated to believe in themselves by faculty and staff, and if they are academically encouraged, they will excel.

Change the Curriculum

Colleges and universities that have been able to change their academic programs to include the experiences of minorities, women, and other excluded groups have done so by cultivating faculty and working in teams. The team approach involves students, staff, and faculty systematically reviewing target curricula to determine what new issues and supportive readings must be provided to students. The University of California at Los Angeles (UCLA) developed a fascinating approach to curriculum change. The campus secured financial resources so that the honors program could buy faculty release time during one quarter to add to their syllabi new readings dealing with the experience of women and minorities in the United States. Making any type of structural change in a curriculum is a thorny problem, as was evident by the debate at Stanford University to consider including non-Western themes. However, the UCLA model provides an incentive for faculty to transform their own courses. Another interesting approach to achieving curriculum change is the Odyssey II Program at Brown University (American Council on Education, 1989). It is an effort that links faculty and students in developing reading lists and creating new courses.

A few words are necessary about ethnic studies graduation requirements. While a required course that will expose all students to the experience of ethnic and racial groups in the United States is a positive step, such a course must be comparative and "substantially consider at least three of the five main racial/cultural groups in American society: African American, American Indian, Asian American, Chicano/Latino, and European American" (Special Committee on Education and Ethnicity, 1989). At many campuses, any discussion about imposing an ethnic studies graduation requirement will bring to light resistance by faculty and students alike. It took one defeat and over two years of discussion before the successful passage of the comparative ethnic studies graduation requirement at the University of California at Berkeley. As increasing numbers of minorities begin to attend U.S. colleges and universities, the curriculum must provide ways to sensitize all students to the experiences these different groups have had in the United States. A thoughtful and well-designed course, taught by an effective faculty, will do much to improve relations among different ethnic and racial groups on campus.

Diversify the Faculty

There will be many opportunities to add more minorities to our faculties. The demographic data on pending faculty retirements and new openings are known (Brown, 1988a; *The University of California in the Twenty-First Century: Successful Approaches to Faculty*

Diversity, 1987). It is not necessary to repeat that discussion. Instead, it is important to mention the development of a strategy that contains priorities and targets for faculty recruitment.

At most institutions, minority faculty recruitment is highly opportunistic. Some institutions set aside one or two positions in a particular school or college for minorities, and at others, the campus commits itself to hire a specific number of minorities over a five- or ten-year period (Stanford and Michigan are examples of institutions that make these concessions). What is needed, however, is a systematic review of the institution to determine what colleges, schools, or departments have an immediate effect on the surrounding community. As for research universities, national priorities involving minority needs must be considered. Then, the president should make available new or replacement faculty positions to these units that should be filled by minorities. Prioritizing opportunities for minority faculty hiring is an important step in diversifying the professoriate (Moore, 1987/88).

Two other issues regarding faculty diversity are important. First, good teaching skills should be an important part of a minority faculty member's portfolio. The ability to reach a wide audience of students is an essential quality for a successful instructor. Second, ethnic- and racial-related research and investigations should not be discounted in the tenure process. If we are ever genuinely to understand each other, we must be able to research and uncover our backgrounds and contributions to American life.

Preparing new minority faculty must be a priority for U.S. higher education. Most of the important steps that are needed to encourage minorities to consider careers as professors have been mentioned elsewhere. However, a few need to be underscored. Recruiting minorities for doctoral programs must begin in grade and especially middle schools. At the undergraduate level planning and preparing for graduate school must be stressed, and students working closely with faculty members who will guide and assist prospective doctoral students is very important. Selecting the right type of graduate program and securing a sufficient financial aid package will be essential to the student (Brown, 1988b).

Several programs identify talented minority undergraduates and encourage them to pursue graduate degrees. The Early Identification Program at the University of Washington in Seattle is a well-designed and operated model (American Council on Education, 1989). Several programs are designed to increase the gender and racial and ethnic diversity of faculty in selected academic fields, and to link financial assistance with employment. Two important efforts are the New Jersey Minority Academic Career program (MAC) and the California State University Forgivable Loan/Doctoral Incentive Program (American Council on Education, 1989, pp. 77–78). A highly successful state program is the Black Doctoral Fellowships provided by the Florida Endowment Fund. Some 25 fellowships provided by the Florida Endowment Fund are awarded each year for doctoral study at Florida public or private institutions (American Council on Education, 1989). At the national level, the Minority Graduate Fellowships from the National Science Foundation, and the Patricia Roberts Harris Fellowship Program in the U.S. Department of Education, provide assistance for traditionally underrepresented students who have demonstrated an ability and aptitude for graduate study in select fields (American Council on Education, 1989, p. 79). These efforts, and others, need to be expanded and new ones developed to ensure an expanding pool of women and minorities for faculty roles in U.S. institutions of higher learning.

Employ Minority Leaders as Change Agents

Academic colonialism can easily thwart an institution's attempts to diversify. Employing minorities in senior leadership positions sends a clear message about the value of cultural diversity among faculty and staff. Far too many institutions hire minorities for senior management roles in "soft" or marginal areas. Hiring them for such positions as dean of students, affirmative action officers, or special assistants to the president for diversity marginalize minorities into professional cul-de-sacs with little opportunity for advancement (Haro, 1990). At many campuses, this tends to trivialize their efforts. Michigan State University and the University of Texas at El Paso have successfully employed minority leaders as academic deans of different schools and colleges. A few institutions have identified and hired promising African-American academic leaders from historically black colleges and universities. These leaders are recruited as change agents. Creative change agents who understand the campus climate and can work effectively with staff, faculty, students, and senior administrators have been responsible for setting dramatic diversity trends. The president and her or his senior executives, however, must be prepared to support the efforts of these change agents and commit the institution to a program of continuing and long-term change.

Two areas that are critical for faculty recruitment are the sciences and engineering. The report of the Task Force on Women, Minorities, and the Handicapped in Science and Technology has some important recommendations for action. There is a coming crisis in the science and engineering work force of the 21st century. The United States faces a shortfall of scientists and engineers that will be pronounced by the year 2000. The projected shortfalls can be met by using our national talent, especially from those groups traditionally underrepresented in engineering and science — women, minorities, and people with disabilities. Without world-class scientific and technical excellence, our international competitive prospects dim. The final report of the task force provides important steps that, if acted upon, will contribute to an improved educational climate and outcome for minorities (Task Force on Women, Minorities, and Handicapped in Science and Technology, 1989).

Reach Out to Off-Campus Groups

Colleges and universities need to carefully study demographic trends in their areas and determine what middle and high schools they will target for recruitment. In some places, particularly inner-city areas, schools are becoming racially segregated (Orfield & Paul, 1987/88). Outreach programs and services must be established with target schools to encourage minority students to consider going to college. Parents must be made aware of the preparation needed for their children to enter college. The liaison efforts with the schools require some important steps: role models need to be identified; the campus must be demystified; and the welcome mat for prospective minority students and their families must be genuine. Local agencies and community groups can be cultivated and work as partners to diversify the campus (Jackson, 1989). Church groups and religious organizations are very helpful in stimulating interest and providing support for minorities to consider college as a realistic alternative. Business and corporate groups can provide motivation, human resources, and economic support.

The STEP Program: A Partnership for the Advancement of Learning at the University of California, Irvine, is a comprehensive effort to work with different groups to improve diversity on campus. It emphasizes interinstitutional cooperation among school districts, community colleges, and four-year institutions to enhance the preparation of minority students for higher education. An important component of this model is the close liaison with parents, teachers, and community groups (American Council on Education, 1989).

Strengthen Ties with Feeder Institutions

It is a well-known fact that 70 percent of the minority students attending college are at two-year institutions. Yet, the rates of graduation and transfer to four-year institutions for these students is disappointingly low. Community colleges must play many important roles for underrepresented minorities. They can serve as hospitable places within local communities to help students develop academic skills. They can provide transitional environments that prepare students for success at four-year colleges or universities. They can rekindle the motivation of minorities who have dropped out of four-year institutions to continue their education. Finally, they can develop or enhance the skills of minorities to be productive members of our society.

An example of a very successful effort to improve the persistence and transfer rate of Hispanics to four-year institutions from two-year colleges is the Puente Project. Initiated in 1982 at Chabot Community College in Hayward, California, its purpose is to reduce the dropout rate among Hispanic community college students and increase the number who transfer from two- to four-year institutions. The program provides community college students with writing instruction; individual counseling in academic, personal, and career areas; and personal contact with mentors from the Hispanic professional community who offer each student a vision of career success and community commitment. It is a program well worth investigating.

These are but a few alternatives available to assist colleges and universities to begin a process for cultural diversity. Numerous guides and handbooks are available that list and describe successful programs. Two need to be mentioned: the American Council on Education's book *Minorities on Campus: A Handbook for Enhancing Diversity* (1989) and the publication prepared by John J. Halcon entitled *Exemplary Programs for College-Bound Minority Students* (1988).

Three critical points need to be stressed that will significantly influence progress toward campus diversity in the future. First is the need for the president of the college or university to be genuinely committed to cultural diversity and change. The president and senior-level executives must have the will to take the necessary steps to diversify the institution. Without their commitment and enthusiasm, faculty, students, and staff will realize quickly that plans and programs for diversity will be praised but not implemented. A lack of commitment may cause such programs to be viewed by minorities as tokenism or lip service, prompting them to use confrontational or sensational tactics. In other places, minorities will vote with their feet and stay away from the campus. Second, if the faculty is not diversified and does not change the curriculum to include the experience of women and minorities in the United States, students will explore other options or may become militant. Third, staff, especially front-line personnel who deal directly with students, must become sensitive to minority differences and needs and learn to work successfully with this new clientele. The president and senior managers, the faculty, and the staff must view diversity as a challenge that offers new opportunities for growth and development. It should be an exciting and cooperative effort that makes people feel good about themselves. In time it will strengthen the active participants as well as the institution.

The inescapable fact confronting us is that the full participation of minorities in all parts of our society is vital to our survival as a free and prosperous nation. Changing demographics in the United States (American Council on Education and Education Commission of the

States, 1988) have made preparing and attracting our minority youth to U.S. colleges and universities a very high priority. Our fundamental goal should be to erase the inequities that characterize the lives of too many minority Americans. Access to our institutions of higher education must be improved for minorities, and programs must be implemented that will ensure their successful participation on the campus as students, faculty, staff, and administrators. The following quote should be carefully considered as we move into the 21st century:

> Perhaps it truly can be said that no other nation on earth, at this point in history, has quite the opportunity that we do to create a fully functioning democracy where all citizens, regardless of race, ethnicity, creed, or sex, can participate completely in all aspects of national life. This dream need not be deferred any longer. Ours is the challenge; ours will be the prize (American Council on Education and Education Commission of the States, 1989).

REFERENCES

Achieving faculty diversity: A sourcebook of ideas and success stories. (1988). Madison: University of Wisconsin System.

American Council on Education. (1989). *Minorities on campus: A handbook for enhancing diversity.* Washington, DC: American Council on Education.

American Council on Education and Education Commission of the States. (1988). *One-third of a nation* (Report of the Commission on Minority Participation in Education and American Life). Washington, DC: American Council on Education and Education Commission of the States.

Beckham, B. (1987/88). Strangers in a strange land: Blacks on white campuses. *Education Record, 68*(4)/*69*(1), 74–78.

Bloom, A. D. (1987). *The closing of the American mind.* New York: Simon & Schuster.

Brown, S. V. (1988a). *Increasing minority faculty: An elusive goal.* Princeton: Educational Testing Service.

Brown, S. V. (1988b). *Minorities in the graduate education pipeline.* Princeton: Educational Testing Service.

Clewell, B. C., & Ficklen, M. S. (1986). *Improving minority retention in higher education.* Princeton: Educational Testing Service.

Education Commission of the States. (1986). *Transforming the state role in undergraduate education.* Denver: Education Commission of the States.

Educational Record: The Magazine of Higher Education [Special double issue]. (1987/88). *68*(4)/*69*(1).

Halcon, J. J. (1988). *Exemplary programs for college-bound minority students.* Boulder: Western Interstate Commission for Higher Education.

Haro, R. P. (1990). Latinos and executive positions in higher education. *Educational Record, 71*(3), 39–42.

Haro, R. P. (1991, January). *Enhancing campus diversity: What not to do.* Paper presented at the annual conference of the American Council on Education, San Francisco.

Harvard Educational Review. (1988, August). *58*(3).

High school graduates: Projections by state, 1986 to 2004. (1988). Bounder: Western Interstate Commission for Higher Education.

Jackson, E. O. (1989). The community and minority students. In M. Odell & J. J. Mock (Eds.), *A crucial agenda* (pp. 49–60). Boulder: Western Interstate Commission for Higher Education.

Jones, A. C., Terrell, M. C., & Duggar, M. (1991). The role of student affairs in fostering cultural diversity in higher education. *NASPA Journal, 28*(2), 121–27.

Kuh, G. D., & Whitt, E. J. (1988). *The invisible tapestry: Culture in American colleges and universities.* Washington, DC: Association for the Study of Higher Education.

Levine and Associates. (1989). *Shaping higher education's future: Demographic realities and opportunities, 1990–2000.* San Francisco: Jossey-Bass Publishers.

Madison Plan. (1988). Madison: Office of the Chancellor, University of Wisconsin.

Minority Recruitment/Retention Task Force. (1989, May). *Minority recruitment, retention and transition: Report and recommendations.* Saratoga, CA: West Valley College.

Moore, W., Jr. (1987/88). Black faculty in white colleges: A dream deferred. *Education Record, 68*(4)/*69*(1), 116–121.

National Task Force for Minority Achievement in Higher Education. (1990). *Achieving campus diversity: Policies for change* (Report). Denver: Education Commission of the States.

Odell, M., & Mock, J. J. (Eds.). (1989). *A crucial agenda: Making colleges and universities work better for minority students.* Boulder: Western Interstate Commission for Higher Education.

Orfield, G., & Paul, F. (1987/88). Declines in minority access: A tale of five cities. *Educational Record, 68*(4)/*69*(1), 56–62.

Rendon, L. I., & Amaury, N. (1987/88). Hispanic students: Stopping the leaks in the pipeline. *Educational Record, 68*(4)/*69*(1), 79–85.

Report of the President's Task Force on Minority Presence. (1989). Moraga, CA: Saint Mary's College of California.

Reyes, M. de la Luz, & Halcon, J. J. (1988, August). Racism in academia: The old wolf revisited. *Harvard Educational Review, 58*(3), 299–314.

Rodriquez, C. (1989). *Educational equity programs at San Jose State University.* Unpublished manuscript.

Special Committee on Education and Ethnicity. (1989). *A proposal for an American cultures breadth requirements.* Berkeley, CA: University of California, Academic Senate.

Takaki, R. (1989). *Strangers from different shores.* Boston: Little, Brown.

Task Force on Black Student Eligibility. (1990). *Making the future different: Black student eligibility* (vols. 1–3). Berkeley: University of California.

Task Force on Women, Minorities, and the Handicapped in Science and Technology. (1989). *Changing America: The new face of science and engineering.* Washington, DC: U.S. Congress.

Turning points: Preparing American youth for the 21st century. (1989). New York: Carnegie Council on Adolescent Development.

University Committee on Minority Issues. (1989). *Building a multiracial, multicultural university community.* Stanford, CA: Stanford University.

The University of California in the twenty-first century: Successful approaches to faculty diversity. (1987). Berkeley: University of California, Office of the President.

WICHE (Western Interstate Commission on Higher Education). (1987). *From minority to majority: Education and the future of the Southwest.* Report by the Regional Policy Committee on Minorities in Higher Education. Boulder: Western Interstate Commission on Higher Education.

II

ACADEMIC
CONSIDERATIONS

5

Reflections on Curriculum Innovation in Higher Education: The New Weatherhead MBA Program

Richard E. Boyatzis, Scott S. Cowen, and David A. Kolb

Managing change in the academic curriculum, in what is taught and how it is learned, must rank among the top 21st-century management challenges for higher education. Universities today often find it easier to build buildings and increase endowments than to bring about fundamental improvements in the teaching and learning processes. The University of Michigan's National Center to Improve Postsecondary Teaching and Learning states that curriculum revision currently takes an average of five years to complete (Genthon, 1989). If we assume that the programs thus revised are not revised again for 5 to 20 years, we see that currently the fundamental knowledge base communicated to students changes in a 10- to 15-year cycle. This is too slow for the pace of the 21st century.

A shorter curriculum revision cycle is not enough, however, to respond to the learning requirements for individuals in the world society of the 21st century. There is a need for innovation in the learning process. Ernest Boyer (1987), president of the Carnegie Foundation for the Advancement of Teaching, has imagined the sorry state of the telephone if AT&T had invested as little in communication research and development (R&D) as higher education has invested in R&D on learning. Increased productivity in learning is essential if higher education is to keep its leadership role in developing human potential.

We cannot, in this chapter, offer a review of curriculum change processes in the many disciplines and professions and unique university settings that comprise higher education, nor can we catalog the many innovations now occurring in the educational process. Instead, we offer the attempt by ourselves and our institutions to grapple with these issues as a case study of some of the opportunities, problems, and dilemmas we have experienced. Our purpose is to reflect on the process of curriculum innovation as it occurred in our institution to see if there are any lessons to be learned that might apply in other areas of higher education.

PREPARING THE ORGANIZATION

In academic organizations successful curriculum change normally represents one element in the organization's total change initiative. Awareness of the need for curriculum change, as well as the initiative to start the process and see it through to fruition, are most effectively accomplished within the context of a comprehensive long-term strategy for transforming the organization. Developing this strategy and gaining its acceptance and ownership by the faculty are the key elements in properly preparing the organization for any type of change, especially change relating to the core faculty activities of teaching and research. It is important to envision strategy formulation as a process of dialogue in which faculty members engage one another on the future of their organization and eventually articulate the philosophy, values, ideas, and vision that will guide the future development of all aspects of the academic enterprise. Without such a framework, there is no organizational context for evaluating the desirability of specific change recommendations.

It is often difficult to locate the beginning of the process of strategic formulation or to determine when the organization is properly prepared to implement the key components of the new strategy. At the Weatherhead School of Management (WSOM) it took seven years before we were able to seriously consider a significant change in the MBA curriculum — an exceptionally long period of time, even for institutions of higher education.

We see six factors as responsible for this lengthy period of preparation. First, this was the first attempt in the history of the school to engage the entire faculty in developing a comprehensive, long-term strategy. Second, the faculty experienced difficulty in making the transition from a disciplined focused mentality to a schoolwide perspective. Third, related to this shift, it was difficult for the faculty to make a commitment to transformative versus evolutionary change. The initial reaction of the faculty to strategic planning was to have the organization do more of what had been done in the past, rather than consider new and significantly different modes of thinking and acting. Fourth, an inadequate number of faculty members and administrators were willing to assume strong leadership for the planning effort. Fifth, the planning process, when first begun, was not linked to the entire faculty. In essence, strategy formulation was delegated to "position-related" faculty, and, consequently, the process was seen as an administrative activity rather than a core task of the faculty. Finally, no stakeholders outside of the organization were involved in the strategic planning effort.

Even under ideal conditions, developing a reasonably well articulated and accepted strategy for an organization would probably require at least two to three years of effort before serious attention can be focused on the process of curriculum change. However, the time spent in the strategy formulation stage will save time and frustration later, as well as increase the potential for the development of a plan for significant and successful curriculum change. Based upon our experience, an organization engaged in the first cycle of significant change should expect to devote three to five years preparing itself for transformation and another five years implementing its strategy, for a total of 8 to 10 years. We believe that subsequent change cycles will require less time because the organization has gone through the planning-learning cycle and experienced a process of continued learning throughout the initial cycle of change.

PROGRAM DESIGN PRINCIPLES

The new WSOM MBA program emerged over a five-year period, culminating in critical faculty votes in May and December of 1989. Throughout the five-year process a number of principles guided our discussions. These principles emerged from the strategy formulation process and early faculty discussions about revising the MBA program.

1. The objectives of the new program should reflect the concept of "added value" from all stakeholders' perspectives. The value-added concept, which assumes that the program can contribute more to students' development and growth, caused faculty to focus on what students were learning, rather than what the faculty was teaching. This perspective focused on how the Weatherhead MBA experience was contributing to improving students' knowledge and skills. It did not assume that the current program did not add value to students' capability, but that we could aspire to have an even greater impact. This was a major departure from the conventional wisdom exemplified by the expression, "If it ain't broke, don't fix it!"

There were many stakeholders whose views needed to be considered in the process of revising the MBA program: potential applicants, students, alumni, faculty, administrators, prospective employers of graduates, community supporters, and donors. While the perspectives of each stakeholder group were different, it was assumed that all stakeholder groups would have to be excited about the changes and perceive their added value. For example, prospective and current students are interested in the impact of changes on their employment prospects. Donors, on the other hand, are more concerned with community and national reputation. All stakeholder groups consider educational goals, outcomes, and responsibilities as important.

A challenge during the process was to avoid settling for the lowest common denominator of changes that all groups would accept and to strive for a design that was exciting, distinctive, and effective. Frustration with previous attempts at change and horror stories from colleagues at other institutions created a heavy blanket of low expectations that threatened to extinguish the fires of innovation. The "me too" approach toward an MBA education was discarded, and a concerted effort was made to develop a truly distinctive MBA program.

2. Focusing on desired learning outcomes facilitates discussion within and among stakeholder groups. An orientation toward learning outcomes encourages viewing students and their potential from a holistic perspective. It focuses attention on the student's knowledge *and* abilities (that is, skills and personal characteristics) at the point of graduation. Desired learning outcomes become a focal point for discussions among people from different groups with different values and different responsibilities concerning the student. The orientation and discussion of outcomes often leads to a discussion of outcome assessment. The questions are raised, "What are the capabilities of our graduates in terms of knowledge and abilities? Are they prepared to enter, or re-enter, the work force? Are they capable of the continuing learning necessary for the world of tomorrow? As soon as the measurement outcome appears in discussions, measuring these same characteristics at point of entry into the program becomes an issue. The outcome assessment approach thereby leads to an acknowledgment and respect for the students' expertise and experience at the time of entrance into the program.

3. Faculty should see themselves as "managers of learning" rather than teachers. This principle requires a shift of control from the faculty as sole director of the educational process to a student-centered approach to learning. When students' learning becomes the primary objective, students must have more control over the learning process. They will want to move at a pace and direction suitable to their individual backgrounds, past experiences, personal learning styles, and so forth. Respecting this diversity of capability and allowing for the diversity of future career interests requires that the program be responsive to the unique learning needs of each individual.

The shift of attention from what is taught to what is learned encourages an overview of the whole MBA program, not merely the courses in it. The shift of the role of faculty members from teachers to managers of learning leads to a shift in the faculty members' thinking, from an exclusive focus on their discipline to a focus on the role their discipline plays in management jobs. The program involves courses, but also relationships with students and other faculty members, extracurricular activities at school and activities at work. All of these experiences are opportunities for learning and development. Although encouraging an individualized program, students should experience membership in the learning community of WSOM and Case Western Reserve University.

This shift in perspective also raises the need for integrative learning. Courses are often effective vehicles for specialized learning, but they may not be appropriate vehicles to foster integration of learning. In the new program we sought to help students find perspectives to integrate what they are learning in different courses, activities to link theory and practice, and opportunities to understand themselves and articulate their career direction. Vehicles for integrative learning are especially useful for currently employed MBA students. Whether full-time or part-time, students often do not have the time or the opportunity to explore what they are learning in their current jobs.

4. Professional graduate education should be liberalizing for the students, getting them to think about issues and situations in new and novel ways and to develop habits of the mind that stretch and expand their capacity to think and act creatively. Many of us are concerned about the increasingly vocational and specialized nature of not only professional education but of higher education in general. As the world becomes increasingly complex, and as organizations operate in vastly different markets, cultures, and economies, managers must be able to think in highly complex, global ways. The natural tendency of professional education is to socialize the person into the profession. This process involves learning to think and act like a person in the field and learning the values and norms of the profession. While this socialization is a valuable aspect of becoming a professional and the goal of every eager aspirant, any profession can become so specialized in its jargon, values, and norms that it excludes innovative thought, sensitivity to new situations, and the learning skills necessary for continued professional growth and development. Since managers must work with people, and the work force is becoming increasingly diverse in most countries, management education should be liberalizing and expand students' views about the global society in which we live.

5. The new program should use state-of-the-art adult learning technologies. Eight adult learning technologies were considered by the faculty during the curriculum change process: competency-based assessment, learning contracts, learning teams, experience-based learning, lifelong learning, machine technology (computers, video),

credit for prior learning, and advanced professional studies. As described in other portions of this chapter, the faculty ultimately used all of these technologies, with the exception of the last two. The early discussion of new program possibilities began with the acknowledgment that the faculty should strive to adapt and adopt new methods of learning, especially those developed for use with adult students. Adult students have some, or often a great deal of, work and life experience. They have well-developed values, opinions, and thought processes for dealing with issues at work or home. To learn a different way of thinking, these students must be given the opportunity to examine their current way of thinking; assess its value, costs, and benefits; explore the new way; and determine its relevance or potential in their lives or work. In professional education, the aim is to help them interpret their experiences and learn new and hopefully better ways to approach these situations in life and work. They must unlearn some past practices, or possibly relearn approaches discarded earlier in life.

6. The curriculum change process should be led by the faculty. Of all of the stakeholders, the faculty is involved in the school and program for the longest duration and has the greatest impact on student learning. If the faculty does not see the benefits and feel the excitement of the change process and the new program, it will be doomed to death from apathy. The faculty must be involved in and primary leaders of changes in the new program to ensure its real implementation, as contrasted to a change in labeling and packaging without a change in content and process of education. To operationalize this, the faculty leadership, the elected Faculty Council, appointed an MBA Objectives Committee (MBAOC) comprised of senior faculty and representatives of the school's six departments. Its charge was to develop a consensus program proposal in coordination with other stakeholder groups for approval by the Faculty Assembly.

7. The proposed program should be resource-consistent with the current program. Since no increase in enrollment was expected or desired, the school's budget would remain relatively the same. In addition, with two-thirds of the faculty tenured, it was clear that whatever program components were identified and developed, they would be implemented primarily by the current faculty. Thus, the current budget and the current faculty would have to be capable of implementing the new program.

DESCRIPTION OF THE NEW PROGRAM

Intellectual Themes

The design principles reflect a number of philosophical beliefs guiding the new MBA program. In addition, we developed an intellectual theme connecting our courses, other developmental activities, and learning environment within the WSOM. The theme is: Creating economic, intellectual, and human value. This is pursued through the four subthemes: managing in a complex, diverse, and interdependent world; innovating in the use of information and technology; developing the manager as leader and team member; and stimulating professionalism, integrity, and social responsibility.

Components in the Program

The new MBA program has six key elements: the managerial assessment and development course, the learning plan, the core courses, executive action teams, perspectives courses, and advanced electives. Every entering MBA student is required to begin with the managerial assessment and development course, which teaches students a method for assessing and developing the knowledge and abilities relevant to management throughout their careers. The output of this course is distinctive from other "assessment centers" in three ways: First, current level of knowledge (that is, the subject matter of the 11 disciplines in the WSOM) and current abilities (that is, the 22 abilities related to managerial effectiveness [Boyatzis, 1982]) are assessed. Second, students are engaged in the assessment activities for about three weeks, followed by seven weeks in feedback and interpretation activities, and then four weeks in developing their learning plan. Classes are held once a week for three hours per class, in contrast to most assessment programs, which spend several intensive days in assessment and less than half a day in feedback processes.

Third, the assessment and feedback process is most effective when experienced in a psychologically safe, social context in the first week of the course. Students are formed into executive action teams of 12 randomly assigned students, with an advanced doctoral student as facilitator. Most of the course activities are conducted in their team.

The executive action team will continue to meet during the following semester as a vehicle for integrating across-course learning; learning from other types of experiences, such as internships, mentorship, and clubs; and to engage in skill development workshops. Each executive action team will have a Cleveland area executive as an advisor. It is expected that involvement in the team will develop the ability to work with others in groups.

There are 11 required core courses, covering the range of knowledge areas typical in management education. They are: accounting, labor and human resource policy, management information and decision systems, managerial economics, managerial finance, managerial marketing, managerial statistics, operations management, organizational behavior, policy, and quantitative methods in management. Each of these courses were revised to reflect the integrative, intellectual themes of the program as described earlier.

There are three perspectives courses in the program; students are required to take at least two of them. They are: managing in a global economy, the history of industrial development, and technology management. These course are multidisciplinary, developed and taught by a team of faculty from at least two departments within the WSOM and one department from another school within the university. One of the objectives of these courses is to provide students with a liberalizing experience by exposing them to modes of thought and materials not typically covered in professional management programs.

Observing the Process of Change

Developing the concept and implementation of change appeared to be successful in that: all stakeholders were excited and almost unanimously in favor of the new program; implementation is proceeding on schedule; and all stakeholders are still excited about the new program. A chronology of events is shown in Exhibit 5.1.

Participation was a key factor. Multiple efforts were made to involve all of the faculty, from the 15 MBAOC members to the WSOM faculty (through discussions at every assembly meeting), to the numerous task groups. Nine task groups were formed to develop the components identified and endorsed by the faculty in their unanimous vote in May 1989. All stakeholder groups were engaged in various discussions at each stage in the process. The style used for all such discussions was open, inviting people to state objections and ideas. Faculty, staff, and administrators were invited to participate in any MBAOC and task group meetings. An important aspect of participation was the use of methods of discussion that suited the faculty culture at WSOM. Most of the analyses began with the collection of data. Discussion would always proceed with analysis of raw data, and then determination of conclusions. Given the quantitative orientation of the faculty at WSOM, this approach proved inviting and provocative, and allowed for full participation.

Patience and perseverance went hand in hand as key elements in the process. Patience was required to wait for people to join the process and become engaged in the excitement. There were many meetings; MBAOC met formally 33 times, involving approximately 1,050 hours of faculty time. Task groups, departments, other stakeholder groups, and full faculty meetings involved an immense amount of people's time. Everyone who wanted to be heard and every idea or issue was given attention. In this process, efficiency is an

EXHIBIT 5.1
Chronology of Key Events

1979–80	Formation of a Strategic Planning Committee; effort failed
1983–85	Series of meetings of full faculty regarding planning resulting in a draft position paper on the WSOM's vision, aspirations, and strategic initiatives; new dean and department chairs take office during this time
1985–87	Discussions begin on desire for change; tone set for thoughtful and comprehensive discussions
January 1988	MBAOC formed to conduct study of faculty objectives
May 1988	Curriculum committee proposals not endorsed in favor of more dramatic changes
August 1988	Subgroups begin brainstorming and identify possible changes
September 1988	Management education conference; feedback of faculty objectives study
November 1988	Visiting committee endorses concepts and activities as impressive
December 1988	Objectives of new program written and endorsed by full faculty
February 1989	Plan for May 1989 faculty vote on new program established; progress reports to faculty begin; reactions from departments to concepts first solicited
May 1989	Eleven core required courses decided; informal meetings about proposed program; full faculty vote to endorse new program
June 1989	Nine task groups formed to develop new program components; intellectual themes developed
December 1989	Final faculty vote to implement the new program in August 1990

enemy. A misplaced sense of objectives may have resulted in merely discovering what was to be done in the new program (that is, design changes) and developing these changes, rather than considering the involvement and commitment of all stakeholders, which is the most important objective.

Perseverance with regard to the overall objectives was vital. Deadlines created internal benchmarks. Using whatever momentum was available was also an important element of perseverance. Momentum was provided by the reaction of WSOM's Visiting Committee (an advisory board of chief executive officers) to initial efforts; it was impressed and encouraged continued progress. A management education conference held in September 1988 was crucial in providing momentum as well as a wider perspective for our deliberations. Deans and senior faculty members from many highly regarded schools of management presented their thoughts, praise, and criticism of MBA programs. The conference ended with a half-day discussion of the WSOM faculty's objectives regarding knowledge and abilities in our courses. This discussion was led by the MBAOC who reported on the study of faculty objectives. The conference presented the WSOM faculty with a sense of the possibility to be different and distinctive from other schools. Another source of momentum was a pilot program begun in August 1989 involving a small number of entering part-time students. It provided encouraging information about their reactions to participation in elements of the new program. Another large boost to momentum was generated by the *Business Week* book and article on business schools, in which WSOM was cited as one of the three most innovative programs in the country, and one of the schools likely to break into the top 20 business schools in coming years.

The politics of knowledge was essential to consider in the process. Efforts were made repeatedly to work within the existing power structure of the departments. Within the MBAOC, the faculty and administrators learned and respected each other's epistemologies and autonomy. Department chairs were often asked to discuss particular proposals or ideas within their departments and to report back to the MBAOC with their reactions and thoughts.

The politics of knowledge was a factor that could also explain several compromises. There was a lengthy debate regarding the number of required core courses, with groups of faculty wanting to reduce the number to five, six, nine, or eleven. All positions involved a reduction from the 14 core courses then required. The compromise consisted of each department or division having one required course in the new program.

Another compromise was the development of the concept of two MBA programs: the regular program requiring 60 hours of course work, and a short program requiring 42 hours. Previously, students could waive any required course if they proved to the faculty of the department or the admissions committee that they had taken a comparable course at another accredited business school. This resulted in numerous negotiations as to length and cost of a student's program. Given the most frequent patterns of courses taken, it has been determined that most of the students will fit into the 60- or the 42-hour programs. Now if a student waives any required course, he or she is able to take an additional elective. This decision removes the discussion from the time and money negotiation and replaces it with a discussion about learning and career appropriateness.

A number of operational practices helped the work of the MBAOC. The objectives of the entire effort were often repeated as a touchstone for meetings and discussions. Staff work was conducted to facilitate discussions at each meeting. A memo would be issued with minutes of the prior meeting, including any decisions or assignments made, or ideas generated. A memo was also issued to all committee members prior to each meeting highlighting the agenda items and providing documentation or thought pieces for their consideration. These memos provided a group memory and helped to minimize rediscussion of issues already covered. Since the committee meetings tended to be two or three hours long, lunch was provided to induce prompt attendance and create the impression that the meetings were not intruding into protected time.

The committee often broke into subgroups to conduct various studies or brainstorm ideas for discussion at future meetings. The staff work involved at least three studies of student and alumni views, two studies of other schools' approaches to issues, two studies of student outcomes, a study of graduation patterns, and the study of faculty objectives.

Information about the progress of the committee was made available to all faculty and administrators through progress memos and presentations at all faculty meetings. These progress memos and presentations were also a stimulus to the MBAOC to bring deliberations to a temporary close and take positions on various issues.

GENERALIZATION AND COMPARISON

Throughout our efforts to revise the MBA program we have been encouraged by the similar work of our colleagues around the world. Before we began, we were inspired by the model of Alverno College. Through its innovative use of assessment in the liberal arts curriculum, this small Roman Catholic women's college has, in less than 20 years, moved from the brink of extinction to one of five U.S. institutions most frequently cited by academic deans as having a successful general education program (Magner, 1989).

Later, we searched for models applying state-of-the-art methods of adult learning to management education. The International Management Center in Buckingham, England, gave our faculty the model of an MBA curriculum based on the principles of action learning (Revans, 1982). Other institutions that had gone through a process of curriculum innovation in graduate professional education similar to what we were attempting helped confirm that we were on the right track. DePaul University's School for New Learning had created a liberal arts professional degree based on self-assessment, learning plans, and group-based learning (Justice & Marineau, 1988). In Australia, the Royal Melbourne Institute of Technology had built an MBA program using competence-based learning, learning teams, learning contracts, and experiential learning (Prideaux & Ford, 1988a, 1988b). Hawksbury Agricultural College had reorganized its entire curriculum according to the principles of experiential learning (Packham, Roberts, & Bawden, 1989).

Faculty from these schools have written extensively on their programs and in some cases about their process of curriculum revision. This concluding section proposes six tentative generalizations about the process of curriculum innovation in higher education based on these writings, our personal familiarity with their efforts, and our experiences at Case Western Reserve University.

1. Curriculum innovation seems to be initiated by strong environmental signals from stakeholders. Linking curriculum innovation to a strategic planning process is one way to sharpen and clarify these signals. Indeed, curriculum change may be difficult, if not impossible, without an established and reasonably well accepted strategic context. Ideas, aspirations, and vision, no matter how vague, are the point guards for change, providing a focal point for dialogue among stakeholders.

Curriculum innovation as opposed to revision may require a transformative, distinctive strategy, rather than the common "me too" strategy of modeling after the top schools in one's field.

2. The view that the faculty have primary responsibility for the academic curriculum is accepted widely in higher education. Successful curriculum innovation requires that this responsibility be translated into responsible, effective action. Collective, cooperative faculty involvement across disciplinary lines is essential for this to occur. Management processes that give voice to diverse viewpoints and promote consensus decisions work best. This takes time, so patience, perseverance, a positive attitude, and tolerance of politics are key.

3. Strong leadership is necessary to manage the change process — not only vision-oriented, involved leadership at the top, but broad and deep leadership in the system. Strategy formulation and curriculum change require the cooperation of the entire faculty and are dependent on the existence of a diverse group of leaders. These leaders play a variety of important leadership roles, such as idea champion, process leader, political negotiator, or cooperative team member. Leadership must also represent the formal departments and the informal coalitions in the school. Trustworthiness and credibility are important assets for anyone involved in leading the curriculum change process.

4. All of the curriculum innovations mentioned involved moving from a teaching to learning perspective on education. The key aspects of this transition involved moving toward an outcome orientation, toward individualized learning and to the creation of a productive social context for learning. An outcome-oriented perspective on curriculum definition has two advantages: First, by defining the curriculum by learning outcomes, the processes for achieving those outcomes are freed from innovation. Current practice controls the

curriculum by controlling the process — through the academic credentials of the teachers and the number of contact hours with them. The fact that in most universities student contact hours are used to determine faculty workload and department size introduces tremendous rigidity in the curriculum as fears of job security and departmental survival are easily raised by suggestions of change. Second, curriculum outcome models such as those developed through competence assessment (Boyatzis, 1982) provide a language for dialogue among stakeholders in the educational process about the purposes of education.

Individualized learning is particularly important for the diverse student population of the future. In the new Weatherhead-MBA, student learning goals and learning methods are individualized through developmental assessment and learning plans or contracts. The social context of learning in the teaching perspective often inhibits rather than enhances student learning. The hierarchical one-way communication of the traditional classroom is not as efficient as structures like learning teams that enhance peer learning and two-way communication between faculty and students.

5. Curriculum innovation is enhanced by the creation of integrative mechanisms in the learning process. In current practice, the curriculum is fragmented and specialized, many pieces often from different puzzles. Integration of learning is left to the student. Examples of integrative mechanisms in the new WSOM-MBA are the intellectual themes, the perspective courses, the assessment and development course and learning plan, and the executive action teams.

6. Successful curriculum innovation results in movement toward a norm of continuous improvement. We and our colleagues feel the new Weatherhead MBA program that emerged from our consensus-oriented faculty deliberations marks a considerable improvement over the old program. We are also aware that political compromise, market realities, and the failure of some good ideas to gain acceptance prevented the new program from being even better. While there is some concern that the new program will be cast in concrete for 10 years as institutional attention shifts to other programs and priorities, we see a new spirit and attitude emerging to resist this ossification.

We borrow the powerful concept of continuous improvement from the quality movement to highlight this encouraging result of curriculum innovation efforts. The idea that curriculum revision and innovation is a continuous process is our best hope for coping with the pace and growth of 21st-century knowledge. We have seen this spirit of continuous improvement on the energetic and exciting campuses of other schools we have mentioned, particularly at Alverno College and Hawksbury Agricultural College.

In our own case, we are not as far along as these sister institutions. As of this writing the new MBA program has not yet begun, but the spirit of continuous improvement is definitely present as we go about operationalizing our decisions in pilot courses and program plans. The lines of communication opened during the change process across departments, between faculty and administration, and among stakeholders have made dialogue more frequent and easier. The sense of accomplishment we feel and the positive acceptance of the new MBA program by our stakeholders (based on advance publicity about the new program, applications are up 90%) stimulates a we-can-do-it-better attitude. The idea that the promotion of learning is the mission of higher education is itself an inspiration toward continuous improvement. Learning is not just for students anymore. Our future requires that we also promote organizational learning and continuing professional development for ourselves and our colleagues.

REFERENCES

Boyatzis, R. (1982). *The competent manager: A model for effective performance.* New York: John Wiley & Sons.

Boyer, E. L. (1987). *College: The undergraduate experience in America.* New York: Harper & Row.

Genthon, M. (1989). Why does it take forever to revise the curriculum? *Accents.* Ann Arbor: University of Michigan: NCRIPTAL.

Justice, D., & Marineau, C. (1988). Self-assessment: Essential skills for adult learners. In P. Hutchings & M. Wutzdorff (Eds.), *Knowing and doing: Learning through experience* (pp. 49–62). San Francisco: Jossey-Bass.

Magner, D. (1989, February 1). Milwaukee's Alverno College for 16 years a pioneer in weaning students from dependence on teachers. *Chronicle of Higher Education, 35*(21), A10–12.

Packham, R., Roberts, R., & Bawden, R. (1989). Our faculty goes experiential. In S. Weil & I. McGill (Eds.), *Making sense of experiential learning* (pp. 129–49). Philadelphia: SRHE Open University Press.

Prideaux, G., & Ford, J. (1988a). Management development: Competencies, contracts, teams and work-based learning. *Journal of Management Development, 7*(1), pp. 56–68.

Prideaux, S., & Ford, J. (1988b). Management development: Competencies, teams, learning contracts and work-based learning. *Journal of Management Development, 7*(3), pp. 13–21.

Revans, R. W. (1982). *The origins and growth of action learning.* London: Chartwell-Bratt.

6

Student Assessment: A Proactive Response for the 21st Century

Serbrenia J. Sims and Ronald R. Sims

One recent higher education reform movement likely to dominate at all types of colleges and universities into the 21st century is the student outcomes assessment. Since the 1986 publication of the National Governors' Association report *Time for Results,* which urged state governments to require their institutions to develop assessment programs to measure what students were learning, some 40 states are now requiring some type of student assessment. One might ask, what is student assessment? According to some the term means the determination of the skills and caliber of students entering an institution. This is primarily the assessment of prior learning in preparation for college-level course work or for remediation. To others, the term is the measurement of college-level learning after one, two, or three years of college. Junior examinations, as used in Florida, is an example of this idea of postsecondary assessment. Finally, a third meaning, and probably the most widely used, is a measurement of college outcomes — of what students learn when they graduate. The third interpretation of assessment places emphasis on the outputs or impacts of education, as opposed to the inputs into the education system (Brown & Faupel, 1986). For this chapter, assessment will be defined as "any process of gathering concrete evidence about the impact and functioning of undergraduate education" (Boyer & Ewell, 1988, p. 1).

Although the definition is simple, it encompasses a variety of assessment activities that occur at diverse cross-sections of colleges and universities in the United States. According to 1990 *Campus Trends* survey findings released by the American Council on

Education (ACE), assessment initiatives at institutions of higher education occur in the following proportions:

Two-year colleges	88%
Baccalaureate colleges	76%
Comprehensive	83%
Doctoral universities	68%

The increased emphasis on student assessment establishes three challenges for assessment personnel in institutions of higher education as we approach the 21st century. The first challenge is to collect data that can help students enhance their learning potential and make meaningful choices about careers, programs, and courses. The second challenge is to aid in the evaluation and improvement of instruction, courses, programs, and the institution itself. The third challenge is to make the college or university accountable to its constituents: students, their families, government, and the public (McIntyre, 1989).

This chapter contends that viewing student assessment programs from a historical perspective will better prepare institutions of higher education to develop proactive, effective, and relevant responses to calls for increased institutional effectiveness in the coming decades. Therefore, this chapter will present a brief historical background on student assessment, review the present status of student assessment at institutions of higher education, and conclude with some recommendations on where student assessment programs should be going to meet the challenges of the 21st century.

STUDENT ASSESSMENT:
A HISTORICAL CONTEXT

"Does the outcome [of a college education] bear the impress of a clear, consistent and valid purpose? Does the thing prove as education to have been worthwhile?" (Flexner, 1908).

These questions asked by Abraham Flexner in 1908 provide a historical context for student assessment and point the way for earlier methods of determining educational quality, such as comprehensive examinations taken at the end of the senior year. Flexner's determination to reform U.S. higher education became more intense as the Great Depression of the 1930s gripped the country economically. During this period, accountability questions posed by Flexner in 1908 resurfaced as government and institutions of higher education became frugal with their resources. In response, various institutions developed sound programs to assess student knowledge. These programs went beyond the snapshot approach, where individual instructors assigned grades to students based on their performance in specific courses. For example, as early as 1928 the University of Chicago used comprehensive examinations to measure student outcomes appropriate to the general education at their college. In 1932, the University of Minnesota followed Chicago's assessment efforts by establishing the General College. The General College's mission was described as "knowing what we are getting for what we were doing" (Eckert, 1943). In 1939, over 25 institutions representing a cross-section of the United States participated in the Cooperative Study in General Education under the sponsorship of the ACE (Tyler, 1947).

As the country began to prosper financially during the late 1940s and into the 1970s, little attention was given to accountability measures such as determining the outcomes of the educational process. In fact, during this time period institutions of higher education (funded by federal and state governments) proliferated at a phenomenal rate to accommodate the growing student body. However, as the mid-1980s approached, another period of economic exigency affected higher education. Thus, attention again shifted to ensuring educational quality. During this formative period two issues dominated higher education: First, at issue for institutions of higher education was the philosophical need and justification for student assessment at institutions of higher education. Philosophical arguments relating to academic autonomy versus governmental intervention were voiced on college and university campuses. In addition many institutions, such as the College of William and Mary, felt that student assessment was not justified given the high quality of students admitted and its national standing (Sims, 1989). However, the impact of three reports: *A Nation at Risk: The Imperative for Educational Reform*; *To Reclaim a Legacy: A Report on the Humanities in Higher Education*; and *Involvement in Learning: Realizing the Potential of American Higher Education* established the need for improvements in secondary and undergraduate education.

A second issue for institutions of higher education that were resisting assessment was financial constraints. Many institutions found themselves faced with state mandates requiring student assessment but with no money to conduct the process. Thus, colleges and universities often took financial resources from other areas within their current operating budget. The 1986 *Campus Trends* survey found that 71 percent of participants felt there were no funds to develop procedures. This problem was virtually eliminated as the assessment movement gained momentum. State legislators appropriated the necessary funds during the budgeting process or offered incentive funding to institutions for their compliance.

With the easing of financial constraints, colleges and universities were now free to investigate important questions similar to those asked by Flexner in 1908. Hutchings and Marchese (1990) identified several questions that individual faculty, departments, programs, and entire institutions faced as they began to tackle the assessment issue:

> What is the college's contribution to student learning? How and what do we know of that contribution?
>
> Do our graduates know and can they do what our degrees imply? How do we ensure that?
>
> To what do the courses and instruction we provide add up for students? Are they learning what we're teaching?
>
> What knowledge and abilities do we intend that students acquire? Do they have opportunities to do so? Are they successful? At what level? Is that level good enough?
>
> How can the quantity and quality of student learning be improved? What combination of college and student effort would it take to achieve higher levels of performance? (p. 14).

These and similar questions served as the foundation for the present assessment initiative.

PRESENT STATUS

Arguments concerning the philosophical need and justification for student assessment and financial constraints at institutions of higher education are no longer the center of assessment controversy. Six years have passed since assessment of student learning re-entered the higher education arena, and now attention has shifted to other concerns such as technical problems associated with the how to of assessment, and political concerns about the uses of assessment results.

Technical Problems

In the 1989 *Campus Trends* survey, ACE found that 68 percent of campus administrators who responded felt that most faculty support the development of some kinds of assessment procedures. More importantly, ACE found that more than 33 percent of those who did respond felt that there were no good instruments available to assess their programs. Thus, attention has turned to locally developed assessment instruments to eliminate some of the technical problems associated with student assessment.

In 1990, 66 percent of colleges and universities that responded to the *Campus Trends* survey were developing their own instruments for student assessment. This figure is up significantly from the 1986 figure of 34 percent. Still, there is room for concern among assessment personnel as we approach the 21st century. Ewell (1989) suggests that one way to further lower this number is to link assessment personnel with the professional measurement community, which can aid in developing tests that accurately measure individual change in addition to tests that measure group change within a student body at institutions of higher education (Warren, 1988; Hanson, 1988). Once the tests are constructed, they should be pre-tested on a random sample of the student population.

A second suggestion for reducing technical concerns is for similar institutions and disciplines to collaborate in designing their assessment programs and measurement instruments. This method appeared as early as 1939, when over 25 institutions participated in the Cooperative Study in General Education under the sponsorship of the ACE (Tyler, 1947). Although the colleges that participated in the study had diverse missions, they felt they would benefit from a concerted effort to study many of the problems they faced. In addition, they believed that despite their differences certain basic problems were sufficiently similar to warrant a united effort. By sharing experiences, materials, and ideas, and by dividing the labor, certain complex problems could be attacked more easily (Tyler, 1947). Such collaboration should be of particular importance and interest to two-year colleges whose primary mission is preparing students to transfer to senior institutions. Since these institutions are not viewed as a final stage in the educational process, they must provide quality education for students seeking admission to senior-level institutions.

Political Concerns

Today's college and university campuses are essentially political entities that must respond to both external and internal calls for accountability. El-Khawas (1989) states that three-quarters of college administrators report their institutions are using assessment information in their internal decision-making process. Externally, each of the six regional accrediting agencies now require some type of student outcomes assessment in its review process. Also, at least 15 states use outcomes measures in their budgeting process, and another 13 have pending legislation, task forces, or commissions responsible for developing an outcomes assessment policy (Bernardin, 1990). Thus, it is important for assessment personnel to respond satisfactorily to all interested parties — both external and internal.

External Accountability

In the 1990 *Campus Trends* survey, 73 percent of administrators expressed strong fears about the misuse of assessment results by external agencies. To further expand on the significance of this data, Banta (1988) points out that policymakers as a group tend to ignore the individuality of institutions as well as the change process that institutions must go through to conduct successfully an assessment initiative on their campus. Not understanding the process, policymakers have suggested that institutions simply adopt the assessment model proven effective at another college or university. In addition, policymakers unfamiliar with assessment often suggest that institutions develop and use a single indicator of quality, when, actually, a complex multi-indicator method often is needed (Ewell, 1989).

Lewis (1988) warns assessment personnel about providing simplified and trivialized information to such external parties as policymakers. He states that the recipients of assessment information may use it to increase their role in making decisions that pertain to higher education, when in fact these decisions would best be made by individual institutions themselves. Although many student assessment programs are begun as a reaction to external calls for accountability, there should be a concerted effort by institutional faculty and administrators to internalize the program. This is the present challenge for assessment initiatives.

Internal Accountability

According to El-Khawas (1989), to date assessment results are used most widely for internal planning purposes. The most popular uses include:

Program and curriculum evaluation	78%
Reports to deans and department chairs	76%
Reports to faculty	73%
Feedback to students	58%

Using student assessment for institutional accountability involves the active inclusion of assessment activities into the everyday functions on college and university campuses. This process, also known as institutionalization, occurs when assessment is incorporated into established institutional practices such as planning, budgeting, student development programming, and comprehensive academic program review (Banta, 1989). If a student assessment program is to be effective over a long term, it is necessary for both academic and administrative officials at an institution of higher education to resist the temptation to view assessment as a one-shot project. Assessment should not be a reactionary process, but should be viewed by those involved as a mechanism for stimulating change at the institution of higher education.

As student assessment programs approach the 21st century most will enter a stage of renewal or decline, depending upon the degree of institutionalization of assessment into college or university functions. As chief executive officers show increased concern with the costs of conducting these programs, many ask if the programs are as efficient as possible in providing maximum return of invested resources. What is being found presently is that assessment results often are placed on a shelf as opposed to being actively incorporated into the university's decision-making process. This should not be continued — if indeed student assessment is to determine institutional effectiveness in achieving the goals and mission of the institution. If a college or university does not successfully incorporate assessment findings into its decision-making process, the program is probably headed for a rapid decline. If assessment results are useful and can be used successfully to justify decisions, then the program will be renewed. Hopefully, before entering the 21st century institutions already will have hurdled the technical and political concerns that presently plague assessment initiatives. Emphasis should then be shifted to the actual inclusion of assessment results into the decision-making process on college and university campuses.

At some institutions such as Alverno College and Northeast Missouri State University, including assessment results into the decision-making process is well under way, but for other institutions just beginning to develop assessment programs and tests, the bond between measures of student performance (within individual departments, programs, and schools) and overall indicators of institutional effectiveness will be at an infantile stage. However, once this bond is firmly established, decisions about goals and resource allocations should be made based on the interpretation of student assessment data. This will involve linking assessment performance with teaching, programming, and student career decisions.

Faculty involvement and support are critical to the long-term success of student assessment initiatives. Faculties at colleges and universities are composed of professionals who generally possess extensive knowledge that can be used to better assessment initiatives. In addition, if faculties are not included in the assessment process, they might respond with open hostility. This hostility might take the form of open or passive resistance to the process. For example, faculty members might claim there is no need for assessment within their disciplines or refuse to attend assessment meetings.

FUTURE CONCERNS

The future of student assessment programs includes increased attention to their usefulness to colleges and universities as well as to external authorities that may have mandated assessment. As student assessment programs begin to generate both good and bad data that may or may not be a positive reflection on the school, it will be necessary to evaluate the effectiveness of the total assessment effort. Such a cost-benefit analysis has a goal of determining whether resources (financial, human, supplies, time, and so forth) have been used both efficiently and effectively at the institution, or whether these resources could have been better used elsewhere.

Institutions will have to spend more time deciding how their student assessment program will be evaluated along with the very earliest planning and design of the program (Hawthorne, 1987; Lenning, 1980). This would insure that all the needed data is collected at the appropriate time before and during the implementation of the assessment initiative. However, with more and more states requiring some type of student assessment information, institutions of higher education are finding that assessment programs are being implemented in a crisis-oriented fashion, resulting in the omittance of critical program evaluations in their initial plans.

Institutions of higher education must also realize that there is often a second inhibitor — financial standing — to the successful evaluation of student assessment programs. Institutions of higher education are finding they must tighten their financial belts at a time when more and more external audiences increasingly are questioning the quality of educational outputs and management techniques on college campuses. One effort to conserve resources has been cutting corners on student assessment programs. Since the evaluation component is not viewed by many as essential to program operation, it is often eliminated. However, evaluation is necessary before improvements can be made.

Tracey (1968) states that improvement of any program can be affected by:

   objective and coordinated evaluation of every aspect of the operation;

   application of imagination and creative thinking by all personnel;

   deliberate collection of the observations, ideas, and thinking of all personnel;

   critical analysis and synthesis of findings, ideas, and alternatives; and

   systematic, time-phased development and try-out of policies and procedures as well as identification of resources (people, equipment, materials, time, space, and money) needed to carry out plans (p. 14).

Student assessment programs should be evaluated by colleges and universities, but the process should not end there. As a final step, the evaluation should include a follow-up plan for the improvement of subprograms within the overall program. The following suggestions may be helpful in preparing the follow-up plan:

Implement changes carefully. Once the evaluation has been conducted, action should be taken to implement some of the changes deemed necessary for the improvement of the student assessment effort. If no changes are made, the resources used in the evaluation were essentially wasted.

Do not try to improve every area at once, which will result in chaos and undue strain on available resources. A reasonable response would be to develop a time-phased plan for improving each subprogram of the student assessment program according to the findings of the evaluation.

CONCLUSION

The success of student assessment programs in the next decade depend upon the specific characteristics of each institution of higher education that implements them. These characteristics include mission, structure, control systems, goals, innovations, and ability to change. For most colleges and universities currently conducting student assessment, the programs generally are hampered by technical problems such as test development and implementation. However, as these programs mature approaching the 21st century, program changes must be tied to ongoing evaluation of the assessment data. At this point institutions of higher education may encounter the most resistance to their assessment efforts.

Despite the reasons for the development of assessment activities on college and university campuses, institutions of higher education must internalize the process. Internalization or institutionalization involves the active incorporation of assessment activities into the everyday functions of colleges and universities. A historical perspective can be used by colleges and universities in understanding assessment programs and for aiding administrators involved in the day-to-day decision-making process. Success in the 21st century will require that administrators respond to increased calls for assessment, outcome measurement, or accountability in a positive, proactive way if they are committed to improving their status in the higher education and surrounding communities.

REFERENCES

Banta, T. W. (1988). Promise and perils. In Trudy Banta (Ed.), *Implementing outcomes assessment: Promise and perils.* (New Directions for Institutional Research Series, No. 59, Vol. 15(3), pp. 95–98). San Francisco: Jossey-Bass.

Banta, T. W. (1989). Waving assessment into the fabric of higher education. *Assessment Update, 1*(2), 3.

Bernardin, H. J. (1990). Outcomes measurement: A review of state policies toward outcomes measurement in higher education. *Academy of Management News, 20*(1), 4–5.

Boyer, C. M., & Ewell, P. T. (1988, March). *State based approaches to assessment in undergraduate education: A glossary and selected references.* Denver: Education Commission of the States.

Brown, G. H., & Faupel, E. M. (1986). *Postsecondary assessment report of a planning conference November 20, 1986.* Washington, DC: Center for Education Statistics, Office of Educational Research and Improvement, U.S. Department of Education.

Eckert, R. E. (1943). *Outcomes of general education: An appraisal of the general college program.* Minneapolis: University of Minnesota Press.

El-Khawas, E. (1989). How are assessment results being used? *Assessment Update, 1*(4), 1–2.

Ewell, P. T. (1989). About halfway: Assessment at the balance point. *Assessment Update, 1*(1), 1–2, 4–7.

Flexner, A. (1908). *The American college.* New York: Century.

Hanson, G. R. (1988). Critical issues in the assessment of value added in education. In Trudy Banta (Ed.), *Implementing outcomes assessment: Promise and perils.* (New Directions for Institutional Research Series, No. 59, Vol. 15(3), pp. 53–67). San Francisco: Jossey-Bass.

Hawthorne, E. M. (1989). *Evaluating employee training programs: A research-based guide for human resource managers.* New York: Quorum Books.

Hutchings, P., & Marchese, T. (1990, September/October). Watching assessment: Questions, stories, prospects. *Change, 22*(5), 12–38.

Lenning, O. T. (1980). Assessment and evaluation. In U. Delworth, G. R. Hanson, & Associates (Eds.), *Student Services: A handbook for the profession* pp. 232–66. San Francisco: Jossey-Bass.

Lewis, D. R. (1988). Costs and benefits of assessment: A paradigm. In Trudy Banta (Ed.), *Implementing outcomes assessment: Promise and perils.* (New Directions for Institutional Research Series, No. 59, Vol. 15(3), pp. 69–80). San Francisco: Jossey-Bass.

McIntyre, C. (1989). Assessment in community colleges. *Assessment Update, 1*(1), 12–13.

Sims, S. J. (1989). *The origins and development of Virginia's student assessment policy: A case study.* Unpublished doctoral dissertation, College of William and Mary, Williamsburg, VA.

Tracey, W. R. (1968). *Evaluation training and development systems.* Washington, D.C.: American Management Association.

Tyler, R. W. (1947). Foreword. In *Cooperation in general education* pp. v–xi. Washington, DC: American Council on Education, Executive Committee of the Cooperative Study in General Education.

Warren, J. (1988). Cognitive measures in assessing learning. In Trudy Banta (Ed.), *Implementing outcomes assessment: Promise and perils.* (New Directions for Institutional Research Series, No. 59, Vol. 15(3), pp. 29–39). San Francisco: Jossey-Bass.

7

A Framework for Developing Market-Responsive Programs in Higher Education

Hugh M. Cannon

Imagine yourself sitting in a meeting of the strategic planning committee of a large urban university. The passing of baby boomers has long since wreaked havoc on undergraduate enrollments. The city has deteriorated, its more affluent citizens having moved to the suburbs, leaving the university's campus isolated as an intellectual and cultural oasis in a desert of poverty and despair. Increasing intellectual demands of the work place have caused graduate enrollments to boom, at least in some areas, but the programs seeking to attract these enrollments have also boomed. The resulting market pressures have left the institution in a financial and administrative shambles. What can be done with dinosaur departments, excess faculty, and vacant facilities? Your committee's task is to address these issues and develop a plan that will ensure the university's viability as it enters the 21st century.

Does the task sound familiar? The specific issues vary from one institution to another, but virtually every college and university has faced or is now facing its own version of the crisis. The crises share a common theme: times are changing, and institutions that are not responsive to these changes are not likely to survive.

PRINCIPLES FOR THE FUTURE

The traditional way of addressing the need for responsiveness is to debate the purpose of higher education. Should it address knowledge acquisition? Intellectual discipline? Vocational education? Education for citizenship? Personal skills development? Character development? Within the constraints of any of these general purposes, should university programs seek to teach theory or practice? The problem is that all of these purposes are important to society. The question is one of priorities. This leads us to four simple but profound principles that are likely to govern the future of higher education in the coming decades.

Limited Resources Require Trade-Offs among Important Objectives

The major issues facing the strategic planning committee arise because no program can address adequately all of the desired purposes of higher education. Limitations in time, student interests or abilities, and financial resources force educators to compromise what they hope to accomplish. For instance, if the university commits itself to an urban clientele, it necessarily must develop programs to meet its particular needs. These programs may be remedial in some respects. Perhaps they include a strong vocational orientation, reflecting students' concern about getting jobs. To the extent that this orientation consumes extra resources, it will interfere with the university's ability to serve suburban students with more traditional undergraduate programs.

Or consider a decision to develop programs that emphasize the learning of factual knowledge. Less time and energy will be left to develop the thinking skills that enable students to use the knowledge. If history majors spend all of their time studying what happened, what time will be left for wrestling with questions of why things happened the way they did? What time will be left for learning a trade? How to vote? How to get along with people? How to be honest and make meaningful commitments.

Programs Must Be Responsive to Their Key Publics

Trade-offs have always existed, but decisions were once made in an environment where educators and politicians were relatively free to decide what was best for their students based on philosophical and political considerations. Now our educational system has become more market oriented. While it is not driven solely by the need to satisfy students, it is driven by the need to satisfy a larger range of public groups with a stake in the educational process, among whom students are certainly prominent. Other relevant publics include parents, actual or potential employers, government officials, religious leaders, and educators. For better or worse, the power of these publics to control critical resources ultimately will determine the ways colleges and universities will respond to be successful in the coming century.

Suppose a university runs an evening program leading to an MBA degree. A major resource-controlling public will be the employers who provide students with tuition assistance. If the university does not respond to the requirements of these employers, students will simply switch to other institutions that do.

Different Groups Need Different Programs

Significantly, resource-controlling publics are not all alike. In fact, there are many diverse segments in the higher educational market, each of which demands an entirely different form of educational program. A careful examination of evening students inevitably will show that some employers fund only programs at accredited institutions; others fund only those whose tuition is within an established range. Some students are supported by tuition assistance and therefore make their decisions based on employer preferences; others are self-supporting and make their decisions based on more personal considerations, such as program content, intellectual rigor, workload, or postgraduation marketability.

To be effective in this environment, the strategic planning committee must ask itself which groups or segments of the market it is trying to address. Deciding whether a college or university program should address knowledge acquisition, intellectual discipline, vocational education, education for citizenship, personal skills development, or character development, or theory versus practice, clearly depends on what segment of the market it is trying to address.

Ability to Meet Needs Depends on Program Design

Unfortunately, developing program purpose is not enough. It does not address the kind of educational activities actually needed by a particular segment of the market. Is the kind of program designed to build knowledge and intellectual discipline different from one that addresses vocational, citizenship, personal, or character-building needs?

The distinction between theory and practice comes closer to addressing the actual kind of education delivered by a program. A theory-oriented program might address thinking disciplines, emphasizing an understanding of general principles behind the way things work. Practice, on the other hand, might emphasize the ability to actually do things more effectively following graduation. For example, a theory-oriented program in psychology would enable people to conceptualize behavior in abstract categories, while one that emphasizes practice would enable them to engage in more effective patterns of behavior.

THEORY VERSUS PRACTICE

Again, imagine yourself in the strategic planning committee meeting. Seldom does a committee of this type progress past the first meeting without having to confront the theory/practice distinction.

On one hand, the market demands programs that prepare students for real life, suggesting a practical, "practice" orientation. People who want a vocationally oriented program want students to learn things that will help them become more effective in their first job. People who support education for citizenship want students to learn patterns of attitudes and behavior that will make them into responsible, law-abiding citizens. People who support programs that develop personal skills want students to become more effective in their ability to communicate and get along with other people. And people who support programs for building character want students who will behave in ways that show integrity and commitment.

On the other hand, many people are concerned that higher education might become too practice oriented and ignore theory in the process. They argue that knowledge acquisition and intellectual discipline should be the primary emphasis, and that these call for less-applied types of learning than do vocational education, education for citizenship, personal skills development, and character development.

In this context, we can define theory as the explanation of why things happen the way they do. Practice is what happens. Those who favor an emphasis on theory tend to worry that a focus on practice teaches students facts or behavior with no generalized understanding. As a result, students will not have the tools they need to adapt their knowledge to new situations.

Those who favor practice tend to be concerned that theory is too abstract or otherwise so removed from reality that it has virtually no relevance to problems students might one day have to face. Implicit in this view is the notion that people can address new situations by looking for similarities in old ones, adapting old solutions to address aspects of a situation that are different.

If the modifications of old behavioral patterns are conscious and based on an understanding of the principles separating one situation from another, then we may say that they are based on theory. The real conflict comes when changes are intuitive and spontaneous. For instance, consider a psychologist who understands every major theory of therapeutic relationships, but who can never think of the right thing to say in an actual counseling situation. Another psychologist may or may not have the same level of understanding but somehow senses the right thing to say when it is needed. What is the difference? Experience? Natural ability?

While education may not do much to create natural ability, it certainly can provide experience. This is the rationale for practice-oriented programs. They provide experience and feedback to students, enabling them to monitor the effects of their behavior and make modifications as needed. Counselors in training might begin by observing experienced counselors, modeling their own behavior on those of their more experienced mentors. Then they progress to settings where they can practice counseling themselves, observing the effect they have on clients and receiving additional critiques from their mentors. Learning from patients' reactions and mentor critiques clearly involves conscious thinking, but the result is an intuitive feel for what makes sense in a given situation. This chapter argues that, to one degree or another, this type of learning occurs in all institutions of higher education and applies to virtually any field, from creative writing, to the analysis of physical stimuli (for example, classifying geological specimens), to the management of human interactions.

One way colleges and universities can address the theory/practice distinction is to identify different types of learning. For instance, one school of thought suggests that educational objectives can be conceptualized in three separate domains: the cognitive, the psychomotor, and the affective domains (Kibler, Cegala, Barker, & Miles, 1974).

The cognitive domain includes objectives relating to conscious thinking abilities (Bloom, Englehart, Furst, Hill, & Krathwohl, 1956). The key objectives from each of these domains are summarized in the first domain of Exhibit 7.1, arranged in hierarchical fashion from least (top) to most (bottom) demanding.

At the lowest level (knowledge), objectives focus on the ability to recall facts, concepts, and theories. This addresses what is probably the most common kind of learning taking place in higher education today. People listen to lectures, read books, and otherwise master the key concepts of a particular discipline, such as the classifications of plants in botany, accepted practices in accounting, or theories of celestial motion in astronomy. At a higher level (comprehension), students learn to understand and make intellectual use of knowledge. They can restate ideas in their own words, translate in language courses, and compare and contrast ideas. The third level (application) addresses the ability to use abstract ideas as a pattern for relating to concrete situations. It is the ability of a law student to recognize the applicability of a legal principle or doctrine to a specific case, or the ability of a computer scientist to use principles of object-oriented programming to develop better computer software.

The next three levels address the highest order of thinking. Analysis addresses the ability to break down ideas into their logical parts and determine the underlying issues and principles, such as a

---

EXHIBIT 7.1
Hierarchies of Objectives within Three Educational Domains

Cognitive Domain

 knowledge, or the ability to recall ideas such as facts, concepts, and theories
 comprehension, or the ability to understand and make intellectual use of knowledge
 application, or the ability to use abstract ideas in concrete situations
 analysis, or the ability to break down ideas into their parts and logical premises
 synthesis, or the ability to develop new ideas from apparently unrelated parts
 evaluation, or the ability to judge the value of ideas for given purposes

Psychomotor Domain

 perception, or the ability to sense objects, qualities, and relationships via sensory organs
 guided response, or the ability to perform a specific act under the guidance of a teacher
 mechanism, or the ability to perform a learned act habitually without guidance
 complex overt response, or the ability to perform a complex pattern of acts
 adaptation, or the ability to alter an act to meet the demands of a new situation
 origination, or the ability to develop new acts through the application of unrelated skills

Affective Domain

 receiving, or the tendency to recognize and pay attention to important stimuli
 responding, or the tendency to act appropriate ways as a result of a stimulus
 valuing, or the internalization of underlying motives that govern response
 organization, or the arrangement of values into a coherent, stable system
 characterization by a value, or the use of values to control one's behavior

---

literature student might do when analyzing the symbolism of a story. Synthesis puts ideas together in new combinations, much as a writer might when composing a story. And evaluation is the ability to judge the value of ideas for given purposes, as students do when assessing the quality of a story they have read.

The second domain in Exhibit 7.1 addressed the psychomotor domain. It includes objectives relating the ability to perform various types of behavior (Simpson, 1974). If we consider this in light of the theory/practice distinction, we might conclude that the cognitive domain represents objectives that would be featured most prominently in theory-based programs, while the psychomotor domain would address more practice-oriented objectives.

At the lowest level (perception), students simply learn to recognize patterns of physical stimuli associated with key behaviors. They then progress from practice with the guidance of a teacher (guided response), to practice without guidance (mechanism), to more complex patterns of behavior (complex overt response).

The highest levels of the psychomotor domain involve the ability to address new situations by adapting old behaviors (adaptation) or by combining unrelated skills (origination). In a music program, adaptation might represent the ability to orchestrate another person's composition, while origination would represent the ability to create a composition of one's own.

The third domain of Exhibit 7.1 summarizes the affective domain (Krathwohl, Bloom, & Masia, 1964). At the lowest level it ranges from the simple tendency to pay attention to important stimuli (receiving) to acting in appropriate ways in response to these stimuli (responding). The higher-level objectives involve internalizing values (valuing), arranging these values into a coherent system (organization), and using this system to govern one's behavior (characterization).

Objectives from the affective domain play a crucial role in many types of education, and yet they do not fall neatly into the theory/practice dichotomy. They address issues of priorities, ethics, and the socialization of students into a particular discipline. In this sense they address practice, but they are clearly different in nature from psychomotor objectives.

This suggests that the theory/practice dichotomy is inadequate, and that institutions of higher education in the coming decades may be better served with a more complex framework for designing alternative educational programs. Let us now consider such a framework.

TOWARD A TAXONOMY OF EDUCATIONAL PROGRAMS

Return to the planning committee meeting. You would like to organize your thinking about the discussion to stimulate new, creative program ideas rather than pointless battles over ideological positions. One approach would be to use the distinctions among high and low levels of the cognitive, psychomotor, and affective domains as a basis for classifying strategic program alternatives. By simply dividing each domain into two groups, we can conceive of programs that seek to serve eight combinations of objectives. These are summarized in Exhibit 7.2.

Type 1 Programs

Type 1 programs involve high-level learning along all three educational dimensions. Typically, a high level of cognitive learning is required as a prerequisite for complex decision making, such as one might be required to exhibit in decision-oriented professions such as business administration or law. In addition, many professional programs seek to socialize their graduates for success, helping them internalize the kinds of values and attitudes that will help them rise quickly in the profession. Type 1 programs go beyond this, emphasizing behavioral skills required for success in the discipline.

EXHIBIT 7.2
A Classification Scheme for Education Programs

Level of Psychomotor Objectives	Level of Cognitive Objectives	Level of Affective Objectives	
		High	Low
High	High	Type 1	Type 2
	Low	Type 3	Type 4
Low	High	Type 5	Type 6
	Low	Type 7	Type 8

The college or university typically develops this type of program to address areas such as medicine and counseling. Students acquire both knowledge and advanced problem-solving abilities. They also are encouraged to internalize values that govern their professional behavior, and they invest substantial amounts of time in actual practice to develop the advanced behavioral skills required for their professions.

Type 2 Programs

Type 2 programs differ from Type 1 only in their lack of emphasis on affective learning. That is, they make no conscious effort to socialize their graduates for success. Perhaps most characteristic of this type would be Ph.D. programs that focus both on theory development and the use of sophisticated research procedures, but that has no established mentor system to socialize students into the academic world of teaching and research.

The institution might want to develop a noneffective program to establish a unique competitive appeal among programs, providing an alternative for those who like a profession but who do not want to perpetuate the established social structure. In Ph.D. programs, for instance, a significant segment of the market may believe the well-established academic attitudes and values regarding research and faculty autonomy are counterproductive to the true missions of higher education.

Type 3 Programs

Type 3 programs involve high-level affective and psychomotor but low-level cognitive objectives. The university might find this kind of program particularly effective in teaching the visual and performing arts. They feature a great deal of practical experience with coaching to help students develop their personal performance skills. The coaching process also provides positive and negative feedback regarding the values and attitudes students express in their learning activities. This is used to socialize students. Cognitive objectives receive little attention because the creative process is seen as intuitive and skill based, not conscious and intellectual.

Type 4 Programs

Many of the more technically oriented visual and performing arts programs fall into the Type 4 category, as would many advanced trade school programs. They teach skills with little attention to the theory or values behind them, beyond facts and concepts and the sense of what things are important and need responses. They are similar to Type 3 programs but without the affective emphasis. That is, they prepare students to perform complex behaviors, to adapt these behaviors to address new situations, and to innovate, developing new patterns of behavior through the application of unrelated skills. The university might use this model to develop vocational programs to address the need for high-quality computer programmers, dancers, or beauticians.

Type 5 Programs

Type 5 programs are very similar to Type 1 programs, except that they exclude high-level psychomotor objectives. That is, they emphasize both high-level cognitive and affective learning. The university might use a Type 5 model to design a rigorous, nontraditional undergraduate liberal arts program, where professors stress high-level cognitive learning and at the same time offer themselves as intellectual role models for the development of intellectual and social values.

Type 6 Programs

Type 6 programs involve high-level cognitive but low affective and low psychomotor learning. If we examine stated missions, most traditional college and university programs probably fall into this category. Many educators see their mission as intellectual in nature. Affective learning is dismissed as subjective and nonscientific. Because psychomotor learning is largely intuitive, it is often dismissed as low level and nonintellectually demanding, therefore inappropriate for teaching at the university level. The result is that any socialization or skill training that takes place in the classroom tends to be more an unintended by-product than a planned element of the program. If students came to the university motivated and already prepared with the skills needed to learn effectively, the university might develop a Type 6 undergraduate program to prepare them for graduate work in the nation's leading universities.

Type 7 Programs

Type 7 programs involve high-level affective, but low cognitive and psychomotor learning. Industry and religious inspirational seminars often fall into this category. While they teach cognitive concepts, many rarely get beyond the knowledge or comprehension levels of the cognitive hierarchy. They often teach specific skills, but these are relatively simple, and the programs encourage students to use them habitually. The seminars use cogent examples and the subtle social cues provided by group leaders and participants to stimulate the internalization and use of values.

The university might use the Type 7 model to develop programs where the kinds of problems students are being educated to solve are relatively simple, where the real challenge is having the values and motivation rather than the skill required to engage in appropriate behaviors.

Type 8 Programs

Type 8 programs involve low-level learning along all three dimensions. This would seem to be the least desirable of all program orientations. In practice, however, Type 8 programs are probably the most common type. They may emphasize theory, but only at the knowledge and concept level. They make little attempt to socialize students into the practice of the subject material beyond teaching students which facts and concepts tend to be more important than others. As with Type 5, Type 6, and Type 7, they make little attempt to teach students specific skills or procedures beyond the lowest levels of the psychomotor hierarchy.

These programs often are more the result of accident than design. Indeed, they may be a natural by-product of two separate phenomena. In both cases, the programs proceed from the same set of assumptions that underlie Type 6 programs, namely that values are subjective and nonscientific, and that psychomotor skills are intuitive and therefore unsuitable for teaching at the university level.

First, the massification of higher education creates enormous pressure for developing programs that are within the grasp of students who often are relatively poorly prepared academically. They do not easily achieve higher-level objectives, especially in the cognitive domain, and so teachers naturally lower their expectations to be consistent with what students are able to achieve.

Second, the increasing importance of research as a mission of high-quality universities has drawn professors who themselves are proficient at the application, analysis, synthesis, and evaluation levels of the cognitive taxonomy, but who see their role as dispenser of the knowledge they have developed. They lecture and require their students to learn the most advanced theories, but students are not taught to derive or critically evaluate the theories themselves. The result is knowledge and comprehension, but little higher-level learning.

IMPLICATIONS FOR PROGRAM DEVELOPMENT

The taxonomy of programs suggested in Exhibit 7.2 provides a useful framework for classifying different types of programs in colleges and universities. One might be tempted to argue that Type 1 programs would be the ideal, but, as suggested by our discussion, this is far from the case. The resource trade-offs make Type 1 programs difficult, if not impossible, to implement. Even if a Type 1 program were possible, many people believe that values and skills should not be taught at colleges and universities. Furthermore, students are not necessarily able or willing to participate in a Type 1 program.

The obvious solution for a college or university is to develop different types of programs to address different needs. Exhibit 7.2 can also serve as a framework for evaluating program options. For instance, we have seen that similar programs have different orientations, such as performing arts programs that emphasize both high psychomotor and high value orientations (Type 3) versus those that emphasize a high psychomotor orientation alone (Type 4). Professional programs, such as MBA programs, typically emphasize a high cognitive orientation (Type 6 model) or a high cognitive and high affective orientation (Type 5 model), but when one considers the interpersonal and communication skills required for success as a business executive, the possibility of moving to a Type 1 program appears very attractive.

In general, the taxonomical framework discussed in this chapter may be used by institutions of higher education to develop programs as part of a three-step process.

Step 1: Needs Assessment

This chapter is not to become embroiled in issues regarding the proper role of higher education, be it knowledge acquisition, intellectual discipline, vocational education, education for citizenship, personal skills development, or character development. All of these are important, but there are necessarily trade-offs. The nature of the trade-offs depends on the students and a number of other relevant stakeholders. They also depend on the nature of the program. Certainly a master of science program in engineering will have a different orientation than a bachelor of arts program in a liberal arts college.

Needs assessment, then, determines the needs and expectations of the relevant stakeholders. This chapter has mentioned students, parents, actual or potential employers, government officials, religious leaders, and educators. An obvious approach would be for a college or university to poll them. We would argue, however, that this is only one of several means to a deeper end.

As a practical matter, the needs assessment stage should almost always begin with interviews of relevant stakeholders. The purpose is not so much to understand needs and expectations as to discover why they exist and how they develop. Generally, there will be several different patterns of response, each representing a different segment of the population. Given that a single program can never service the needs of every segment, the planner might follow up with a poll to determine the size of each segment as one of the criteria used for deciding which ones to address.

Exhibit 7.1 provides a useful vocabulary for describing needs. Exhibit 7.3 provides the structure of a needs assessment matrix that can be used for summarizing the anticipated program needs of each segment. The rows represent each of the educational objectives listed in Exhibit 7.1. The columns represent each of the segments identified through needs assessment research. Each cell should contain a summary description of the key objectives for each segment.

For instance, consider how our urban university might develop its undergraduate program. Suppose that, upon interviewing stakeholders, the planners discovered two major segments. The first consists of relatively well prepared students, virtually all of whom would go on to professional graduate programs. The second consists of poorly prepared students, many of whom would drop out, and with only a few expected to attend graduate school.

The matrix entries for Segment 1 tend to reflect a Type 6 program, emphasizing a full range of cognitive objectives, with content emphasis across a large range of disciplines. The program would focus on the basic knowledge, understanding, and thinking abilities that would serve these students well in life and their graduate programs. The program would leave the teaching of professional skills and values to graduate school.

The matrix entries for Segment 2 reflect a Type 7 program, emphasizing the value orientation these students would need, first to complete college, and second to begin a pattern of success in their jobs once they graduated. The program ideally would include high levels of cognitive and psychomotor objectives as well, but time and

EXHIBIT 7.3
A Needs Assessment Matrix

	Segment 1	Segment 2
Cognitive Objectives	Emphasize the full range of cognitive objectives, with content emphasis across a large range of disciplines, preparing students for more specialized graduate education.	Address lower-level cognitive objectives, focusing on the basic elements of knowledge expected in a standard undergraduate education, supplemented by the basic problem-solving skills needed to successfully graduate.
Psychomotor Objectives	Address lower-level psychomotor objectives, focusing on the ability to perform those tasks that are necessary to a good undergraduate education, leaving higher-level skills to be learned in graduate school.	Address lower-level psychomotor objectives, focusing on the ability to perform those tasks that are necessary for success in undergraduate courses, supplemented special efforts in the areas of writing, oral communication, and interpersonal skills to facilitate success upon graduation.
Affective Objectives	Address lower-level affective objectives, focusing on the ability to recognize and respond appropriately to class material, leaving the socialization process to be learned in graduate school.	Emphasize the full range of affective objectives, with special emphasis on the development of a value system that will motivate students to complete college and succeed in their first job.

resource constraints would limit these to very basic problem-solving tools and communication skills.

Step 2: Developing a Strategic Plan

Using the matrix forces the planner to sort through priorities and summarize the most important types of program objectives for each segment. This sets the stage for developing a strategic plan. Exhibit 7.4 provides a summary of its structure and content.

The background situation section plays a crucial role by setting the governmental, economic, social, and technological stage for the program. It should describe the results of the broader needs assessment, including a full analysis of all relevant stakeholders. This should then be followed with a more specific analysis of the various segments the program might serve, including a summary of the needs assessment matrix analysis.

EXHIBIT 7.4
Contents of a Program Strategic Plan

Section	Content
I. Executive Summary	A short overview capturing the essence of program strategy, along with its key components.
II. Background Situation	Relevant background regarding the institutional mission, the competitive, legal, economic, social and technological environments, and the results of the needs assessment.
III. Program Objectives	Key objectives and specific, quantitative goals regarding: (1) what the program hopes to achieve relative to the overall institutional mission and objectives; and (2) stakeholder needs and expectations.
IV. Program Strategy	The general approach by which the program hopes to achieve its objectives.
V. Action Plans	The specific actions that will need to be taken to make the program work.
VI. Program Budget	Financial projections, including both revenue and expense considerations.
VII. Program Controls	Procedures for ensuring that the program is achieving its stated objectives.

The program objectives section of the plan includes two different perspectives: First, it should describe the objectives of the program from an internal perspective, including specific enrollment and budgetary goals. Second, it should address the objectives the program should achieve relative to its major stakeholders. For example, returning to the example of the state university designing an undergraduate program, program objectives would address the segment actually targeted by the program. If the target segment were the less-prepared students (Segment 2), objectives would include key statements from the needs assessment matrix, such as: "Teach students to recognize the importance of their college education and use this recognition as a motivating force in pursuing their studies." They would also include employer-related objectives, such as: "Provide graduates who are motivated to learn and who value honesty, productivity, and loyalty to their employer." Finally, the objectives would include specific goals regarding program completion rates, student performance, and placement.

Program strategy addresses the educational approach the program will use to achieve its objectives. For instance, the traditional lecture method is relatively ineffective in motivating students to begin using appropriate values to govern their behavior, as they would do in our hypothetical Type 7 state college undergraduate program. The strategy would probably include the use of lectures to address low-level cognitive and psychomotor objectives, but it would need to include methods such as values clarification workshops or behavioral laboratory methods incorporating principles of social reinforcement to address the high-level affective objectives.

Action plans address the specific actions that must be taken relative to curriculum requirements, resource allocations, and management procedures in order to make the program work. It would include hiring requirements and criteria, physical facilities arrangements, and course development, generally outlined by calendar dates.

Budget requirements are relatively self-explanatory although by no means trivial. Indeed, poor budgeting, or just as common, correct budgeting within the constraints of a poorly designed budgetary system is one of the major causes of program failure.

The significance of this becomes apparent in the application of the program controls section of the plan. This section should specify the procedures that will be used for ensuring that the program achieves its objectives. In practice, many of these controls often involve budget variance analysis. Because of financial pressures facing the institution, budget overruns often result in cuts that compromise program objectives. Program controls should include contingency plans for correcting budget variances in ways that will promote rather than detract from program objectives.

Step 3: Program Implementation and Control

One of the most shocking lessons a beginning administrator learns is that the development and approval of a plan does not necessarily mean the plan will ever be put into practice. The final step in program development, then, is actually putting the program into practice and ensuring that it functions effectively. As we have noted, the strategic plan should address the issues of implementation and control. The key task, then, is really one of ensuring that the plan is followed. This requires commitment from the highest levels of administration. The commitment ultimately must express itself in two ways: the actual releasing of funds as needed to carry out the plan, and the enforcement of the administrative procedures specified by the plan, including its periodic review to ensure that key people are aware of these procedures.

REFERENCES

Bloom, B. S., Englehart, N. D., Furst, E. J., Hill, W. H., & Krathwohl, D. R. (1956). *Taxonomy of educational objectives — the classification of educational goals: Handbook 1. Cognitive domain.* New York: David McKay.

Kibler, R. J., Cegala, D. J., Barker, L. L., & Miles, D. T. (1974). *Objectives for instruction and evaluation.* Boston: Allyn and Bacon.

Krathwohl, D. R., Bloom, B. S., & Masia, B. B. (1964). *Taxonomy of educational objectives — the classification of educational goals: Handbook 2. Affective domain.* New York: David McKay.

Simpson, E. J. (1974). The classification of educational objectives in the psychomotor domain. In R. J. Kibler, D. J. Cegala, L. L. Barker, & D. T. Miles (Eds.), *Objectives for instruction and evaluation,* pp. 107–12. Boston: Allyn and Bacon.

8

Teaching as Learning: The Case for Community College Scholarship

Betty Duvall

The purpose of the university has changed, evolved, and expanded since the idea was first conceived in medieval Europe. Throughout the history of higher education, however, the notion of discovery, of advancing knowledge, of passing on to one's students not only information but a love of learning has been implicit. In modern times this activity has been described as research, as scholarly activity, as one's responsibility to one's profession.

In recent years, the responsibility for research and scholarly activity was ascribed to the university and not as clearly seen as the role of community colleges or smaller institutions of higher education. Those colleges were more nearly seen as "teaching" institutions. While university faculties saw their primary duty as research (activities that could be measured through publications — publish or perish), community college faculties eschewed research in favor of teaching. Both groups responded to the third commonly held mission of the university — service — by attaching research to service of a defined community or adding service to the teaching responsibility.

Recently, a remarkable shift in these firmly entrenched ideas has begun. Universities that, their critics charge, pay little attention or give little reward to good teaching have begun to acknowledge teaching as part of their mission. Alumni magazines may feature a faculty member known for good teaching right along with the research recognized through funded projects — and the football team. Good teaching was, no doubt, always there, but its recognition is a somewhat new phenomenon.

Of even more interest, though, is the recent recognition of scholarly activity as part of the proper work of those faculty members outside the research university. Ernest Boyer makes the case for a new view of scholarship by redefining the work of the professoriate into four kinds of scholarship: the scholarship of discovery, defined as what is to be known or found, which is the more commonly viewed pure research; the scholarship of integration, which explores the meaning of research findings or places new ideas and isolated facts in context; the scholarship of application, which is research knowledge applied to problems to be solved; and the scholarship of teaching, which is not only transmitting knowledge but also transforming and extending knowledge and ideas (1990, p. 16). This final definition of scholarly activity is indeed a transformation, an extension of the widely held idea of research. By extending scholarly activity to incorporate teaching, all members of the academic community may engage in scholarship. Funded pure research and discovery evidenced through publication in prestigious juried journals, the realm of the university professoriate, is no longer the exclusive definition. Under this expansion, faculty in smaller institutions and community colleges are also called on to pursue scholarly activities.

TEACHING AS SCHOLARLY ACTIVITIES

Boyer first established the view of teaching as part of legitimate scholarly activity in his review of undergraduate education in the United States. There he commented, "Scholarship is not an esoteric appendage, it is at the heart of what the teaching profession is all about . . . and to weaken faculty commitment for scholarship . . . is to undermine the undergraduate experience, regardless of the academic setting" (1987, p. 13). Seen in this light, scholarly activity is more than appropriate to those many institutions that deliver a great part of undergraduate education in the United States. It is an integral and necessary part of teaching.

The concept of returning to the earlier definition of scholarship encompassing teaching has also been proposed by George Vaughan, a former community college president who has written widely on community colleges. He charges that community colleges will be accepted as truly a part of the higher education community and will leave behind their inferiority complex only when scholarship is fully recognized as part of the community college mission (1988, p. 26). He differentiates scholarship from research by suggesting that "scholarship is the systematic pursuit of a topic, an objective, rational inquiry that involves critical analysis," while "research is a systematic objective search for new knowledge or a new application of existing knowledge" (p. 27).

Vaughan notes five reasons community colleges have not engaged in scholarship: they have failed to link scholarship to teaching; they have failed to reward scholarship; presidents (and presumably other administrators) fail to engage in scholarship themselves; community college faculties and administrators view their professional obligation as to their job only, failing to see a relationship between job and progression; and many community college professionals have been convinced their mission is teaching as opposed to research (1988, pp. 28–29).

The discussion of teaching as a scholarly activity has been further expanded by K. Patricia Cross. Using the term "classroom research" she (and fellow researcher Tom Angelo) are proponents of the teacher-as-researcher, investigating the teaching and learning process as it occurs in the classroom. Taking the precept that community colleges have teaching as their mission, Cross feels that by investigating the teaching act as it occurs, both teaching and learning can be enhanced, and the principal researcher, the teacher, will have, by definition, engaged in scholarship. Cross's idea of classroom research has been welcomed by community college faculty and administrators. The idea is bound to be popular in that arena because it speaks so closely to what community colleges feel is their mission (teaching), it responds positively to recent criticism of education in general, and it provides an acceptable response to calls for accountability both in and outside the institution.

ACCOUNTABILITY AND THE COMMUNITY COLLEGE

Community colleges, since their inception in the early 1960s, have spoken in hushed and emotional tones about the community college as a movement. Tacitly understood in that was the preeminence of teaching, especially teaching those students who otherwise might not have had access to higher learning, those who were found hard to teach by previous educational institutions, and those who had not been successful learners in the past. So, when Cross speaks of the community college students who "will be awakened for the first time in their lives to the immense satisfaction of learning," while acknowledging that "community college teaching also offers the greatest potential for discouragement and frustration of any teaching career frustration because the system is hard on students who can't or won't move with the group, and discouragement because we can't always find the keys that will unlock the universal human potential for learning," she hits on the heart of the concern community college teachers feel (1990). The opportunity to explore how that can be changed through classroom research is most appealing.

Further, recent criticism leveled at all educational institutions accuses educators of failing. Studies such as *A Nation at Risk* show

U.S. student achievement at low levels in comparisons with European and Asian students. This report and others like it resulted in the creation of still other commissions and reports, some national, some statewide, and some local, all joining in the chorus of condemnation. The good news is the realization that an informed citizenry is needed for a democracy to work, and that a qualified and productive work force depends on the educational system. The even better news is that educators want to do something to make education better. Classroom research is a good beginning for an assessment of institutional effectiveness, one that involves faculty members in a nonthreatening way.

Assessing institutional measures of effectiveness has become a major community college issue. Assessment may be mandated by political bodies, regional accrediting bodies, or local boards, or it may be a part of an institution's own quality assurance. The resulting information can serve to reassure faculty, boards, and communities, and can serve as the basis for change in curriculum and teaching methods. As students enter the institution assessment may be used for course placement; to determine student learning and development; as certification and gatekeeping; to improve courses, programs, and services; and to demonstrate institutional accountability.

Assessment may include standardized tests but should not be limited to that. Locally developed measures including qualitative emphasis involve faculty and staff in self-examination, in clarifying goals, and in increasing their sophistication in research methodologies. Assessment should track the intellectual and personal growth of students over a period of time, measure changes in student attitudes and values, and measure the "value added" by postsecondary education — that is, what knowledge and skills has the educational experience added to those the student brought to school.

THE ROLE OF CLASSROOM RESEARCH

Classroom research lets the teacher and the institution respond immediately to those seeking educational reform and accountability. It quickly diffuses the knee-jerk reaction to create tests to measure student achievement by allowing the teacher to both identify the problem and seek a solution, rather than stand by while experts measure, diagnose, and prescribe. It makes the teacher the researcher, the discoverer as well as the interpreter of the data, and the explorer of applied research.

What, then, is classroom research? Why is it the magic elixir that can transform teachers in community colleges and small institutions of higher education into full-fledged researchers and scholars? Cross defines classroom research as "the careful, systematic, and patient study of students in the process of learning, and, more specifically, of how students are responding to our efforts to teach them" (1990, p. 4). More helpful to understanding, however, are examples of classroom research. A tenet is that teachers need immediate feedback devices if they are to access what students are learning from their teaching. One such device is to ask students two questions in the last few minutes of the class: What is the most important thing you learned today? Is there anything we have studied that you feel unsure about, or any questions that remain unanswered? This simple exercise not only gives the teacher immediate information on students' progress, and does so in a timely fashion that allows the teacher to intervene and add to understanding or correct misunderstanding, but it also provides reinforcement for student learning by asking them to synthesize and restate their understanding. I employed this device while teaching a freshman-level humanities course in a community college. Most of the students were adults who would not have chosen to take the course had it not been required in their business administration curriculum. I delighted in getting them hooked on the arts and literature and, from their grades and informal responses, I thought I was pretty good at it. Yet my experience, no doubt, is similar to that of most teachers who try this: I was astounded to learn how little background these adults had in the most basic Western ideas and culture, the sorts of things I had assumed was in their learning experience. I was equally perplexed at how close and yet how far many of the concepts I taught were from the target, like arrows whizzing close by but not hitting the bull's eye of full understanding. Upon that discovery a teacher becomes a confirmed classroom researcher.

Other examples include a brief questionnaire to determine students' understanding of terms, or an examination of students' papers or projects in related courses to see if theories or skills learned in one course are applied successfully in courses that follow. The idea is to integrate research into everyday teaching, an idea confirmed by Boyer's suggestion of the scholarship of teaching. From this review it is evident that scholarship is an important part of the responsibility of the professoriate at all levels, at institutions of all sizes in higher education. Moreover, it seems evident that those who pride themselves on good teaching as a preeminent goal of their profession can enhance that goal through scholarly activities.

SCHOLARSHIP DEFINED

But, what are those scholarly activities? Must scholarship be redefined for it to be applicable to institutions outside the definition of the research university? What are appropriate scholarly pursuits that will influence good teaching directly?

Cahn, in his 1978 book *Scholars Who Teach,* takes a rather conventional definition as he ties scholarship to good teaching: "Writing articles for scholarly journals sustains and facilitates good teaching rather than hindering it, for such scholarship develops a teacher's ability to think critically by leading him to submit his ideas to the judgment of his peers" (p. ix). More recent evidence for a conventional definition is found in quite a different source, a letter from the Modern Language Association (MLA) to the U.S. Senate urging rejection of a nominee for membership on the advisory council of the National Endowment for the Humanities (NEH). As reported in the *Chronicle of Higher Education,* the MLA charged that the nominee lacked adequate scholarly credentials, saying she had "written journalistic book reviews . . . that are not contributions to scholarship, a book chapter that relates personal experiences . . . this is also not a contribution to scholarship, and three essays that are modest pieces of scholarship" (Myers, 1991, p. A3). Sure, the authors of this letter may have had issues other than the proper definition of scholarship in mind, but in invoking the long-held view of scholarship they certainly expected to generate an appeal that would be accepted and rallied around by their constituency.

Nevertheless, as discussed earlier, others in education appear to suggest that the conventional definition of scholarship warrants expansion at the least, massive review at the most. Boyer (1990), in adding the scholarship of interpretation, application, and teaching to the scholarship of discovery, certainly suggests expansion of the definition. Vaughan, in amplifying his definition of scholarship, offers concrete examples of the definition: "Scholarship results in a product that is shared with others and that is subject to the criticism of individuals qualified to judge the product. This product may take the form of a book review, an annotated bibliography, a lecture, a review of existing research on a topic, a speech that is a synthesis of the thinking on a topic" (1988, p. 27). This is hardly research as commonly accepted at research universities. Under this interpretation, the work of the nominee so roundly rejected by the MLA would be quite acceptable.

Vaughan takes his definition even further, linking it to professional growth and development: "Scholarship requires that one have a solid foundation in one's professional field and that one keep up with the developments in that field" (1988, p. 7). Many in the university professoriate would scoff and chuckle at that observation. Is that not assumed, they would think. Is it not too obvious to be said? Apparently not in the community college arena. Can we assume, then, that reading in one's field constitutes scholarship? Or must one do something with what one has read — expand, synthesize, interpret, teach to others (colleagues or students) — to authenticate that activity as scholarship?

Cross, as we have seen, calls on faculties to develop research projects in their classrooms (discovery) and to use that newly found knowledge in improving their teaching (application). She urges careful, systematic study of the impact of teaching on learning. Whether or not this newly discovered information on the impact of its application is shared with others in the field through published articles, papers presented at professional gatherings, or informal chats around the coffee pot is presumably left to the individual researcher. Even so, the admonition to share this newly gained knowledge may be seen as implied if not stated forthrightly.

FACULTY SCHOLARSHIP

While these new views of scholarship are prominent in the literature, how are actual practitioners in the field viewing the role of scholarship in the community college? Are scholarly activities becoming a part of the usual activity of the faculty? Are rewards in place to encourage such activities? If so, how is scholarship defined? To explore these questions, chief instructional administrators in a number of community colleges were asked their views.

Deans and vice presidents of instruction were selected for their prominent role in instructional leadership and management. Instructional administrators representing geographical distributions, large and small community colleges, urban and rural colleges, single campus and multicampuses, were selected for their national leadership roles. When asked if scholarship is linked to teaching they replied, without exception, in the affirmative. While some made delineations between activities at their institutions and those at research universities, and while some indicated a wish that there be more emphasis on or importance given to scholarship, all seemed to feel that active involvement in one's professional field of study enhanced their effectiveness as teachers.

Baccalaureate Scholarship

The activities they viewed as scholarly were very much in line with the new definitions. Several instructional administrators referred first to faculty publications. Examples included members of English departments who have published their own creative writing (poems, short stories, novels). Articles in professional journals were also mentioned; journals may have been juried in some cases but not in all. Others referred to funded projects in which faculty members were engaged: the NEH, the National Science Foundation (NSF), and other federal grants were more likely to be mentioned than were private research grants. Projects were more likely to be related to teaching or curriculum materials development than purely subject-related projects. Still others cited presentations at professorial conferences; again, these seemed to center on teaching strategies and teaching materials development. Several administrators cited classroom research as an example of faculty involvement in research and scholarship. In many instances, this seemed to be an ad hoc relationship rather than a collegewide effort or emphasis; an individual's interest instead of a concerted, defined, and developed effort toward researching the teaching and learning act, with results made available to the total college community. Projects such as writing across the curriculum (in one instance a multiyear study employing control groups) were also given as examples of faculty scholarship.

Not surprisingly, English department faculty and writing projects were mentioned most frequently as examples of faculty scholarship. In many minds, scholarly activities equated with writing and writing teachers come immediately to mind. In addition, this may indicate that writing teachers are actively doing what they are teaching, an effort that not only illustrates scholarly activity but also the impact of scholarly activity on teaching. One administrator, in describing a particular English teacher whom he felt fit the definition of scholar, said the teacher "passionately cares about the field," surely an indication of responsibility felt to the profession.

Other subject areas were also mentioned. Areas such as the humanities, where external funding is available (NEH) and science (NSF — although that agency has received criticism for its failure to fund research projects in community colleges and its focus on funding major research universities). Developmental studies, a major effort in community colleges, was mentioned (related to educational psychology in this instance) along with sociology and accounting. Fine and performing arts, where faculty members frequently recognized the need to make art and to risk sharing their work or performing for the public and critics in order to maintain credibility in their profession and with their students, are other examples of scholarly activity among community college faculty.

Transfer subject areas or general education was the first area to spring to the minds of instructional administrators when asked about scholarship. Perhaps that is to be expected: we in higher education have been taught that scholarship happens in these areas.

Vocational and Technical Scholarship

Yet, baccalaureate education is not the only emphasis of community colleges. In fact, some might argue it is of less importance than technical education, or complain that it has undue and increasing attention. The other important tenets of the community college instructional mission are developmental education;

vocational, technical, and career education; short-term customized training and occupational courses (community education, community services), and student development services. While developmental education was mentioned, this area is likely to grow as an emphasis of community college research and scholarship as colleges are called upon to explain costs and results of remedial efforts.

Technical education is also likely to be an increasingly fertile area for community college scholarship. Community colleges pride themselves on reflecting changes in work force needs, in responding to and reflecting their communities. In no other area of community college education is the change more dramatic and evident than it is in technical and vocational education. The vocational education that powered the success of community colleges in their beginnings early in the 1960s was often skilled trades and preparation for "dirty" hands-on jobs; programs in diesel mechanics, auto body repair, automotive maintenance, building trades, and welding abounded. Community colleges have not foresworn that part of their educational mission. However, the fields themselves have changed. Automotive maintenance now emphasizes electronic diagnostic equipment to determine the repair needs of electronic equipment in late-model vehicles. Course syllabi in diesel mechanics read like outlines for courses in logic, as they prepare students to understand electronic systems. The nature of the materials used in many vocational and technical areas calls into question safety and environmental concerns that require faculty to be knowledgeable in chemistry.

Vocational and technical programs in community colleges also include technical subject areas such as engineering technology, health-related programs (registered nursing, radiologic technology, and so forth), and many other specific programs too numerous and diverse to list here. Further, many of these areas also participate in professional program accreditation. Both influence and encourage faculty participation in scholarship in their fields. The point is, technical and vocational program areas are ripe for scholarly activity and have begun to demonstrate that interest. Instructional administrators mentioned electronics engineering technology, office systems technology, and automotive technology as examples of faculty scholarship. Vocational and technical education students have always had to demonstrate what they had learned by actual on-the-job performance. The "value added" from their educational experience, that part of the assessment trend, has always been an integral part of vocational and technical education. Faculties in these areas have to be involved in how to best teach the requisite skills and knowledge, in how their students could best learn — and demonstrate — skills and knowledge. The concept of classroom research may be new to the baccalaureate teacher, but, in principle, it is not new to the vocational and technical teacher. The term "classroom research" may be new to these faculty members, but the how, the where, the why is not. Vocational faculties have been teaching and testing performance and understanding at the same time, making connections between concepts learned and concepts yet to be learned, organizing curriculum in a progression that students can follow and comprehend, determining what students actually take away from the classroom (as opposed to what the teachers hope they would take away), and emphasizing the process of teaching along with the content of what is being taught. The precepts that Cross espouses in classroom research are part and parcel of vocational and technical education.

Vocational and technical faculty have been involved in scholarly activity as defined by Cross, Vaughan, and Boyer. Perhaps neither they nor community college leaders have recognized it as such or named it scholarly. In addition, those faculties in the sciences and the applied sciences have more closely approached the pure research or applied research of the university. Examples of community college faculty members pursuing research that results in publication are numerous. The research may be in college laboratories, field research, or local industrial labs. The same holds true for applied research projects.

Community Service and Education Scholarship

Community service and education are somewhat harder to measure in their scholarly activities. Lack of such activities might be suggested inasmuch as these courses are frequently taught by part-time faculty members who lack a scholarly community, who are not really part of the academy, and who teach courses that are short-term and highly specialized to a job or company. On the other hand, because they are part-time and have full-time positions in their field, some may be actively involved in advancing knowledge in their profession. Others may be described more accurately as practitioners than as researchers.

When asked, instructional administrators can readily name faculty members on their staff they consider scholars representative of baccalaureate, vocational and technical, or developmental or community service. This in itself suggests that the institution recognizes the value of scholarship.

Yet, what evidence can the institution provide that it does indeed value and reward scholarship? Some institutions weigh scholarly activities as a criteria for promotion. More common, however, are not institutionalized rewards but recognition by the instructional administrator. Such rewards as increased travel funds (especially if the faculty member is presenting a paper), released time from teaching or office hours, public acknowledgment within the institution and outside it (an article in the local paper), or maybe a complimentary note from the vice president or lunch with the president. Most administrators admitted the recognition was not as much as it should be. There is more recognition in some institutions: an annual authors' reception with the presentation of a gift to each author, the selection of the outstanding faculty member of the year for scholarly activity, and an honorarium (funded by the College Foundation) are examples of institutionalized recognition.

If faculty members in community colleges are to feel that scholarship is an integral part of their responsibility, then new faculty members should be told this when they are hired. There is little evidence of this in community colleges. Faculty members in a department that values scholarly activity are likely to make this known to new members and to select members who also hold this value. Departments that do not see scholarship as important to the community college are, obviously, likely to present that view and select accordingly. Because scholarship is not fully a part of the community college culture, administrators are least likely to tell new faculty members this is a part of the institution's expectations. During their orientation new members may be introduced to the concept of classroom research or related topics important in good teaching and assessment. In general, scholarship is up to the individual; either the individual sees a responsibility to the profession and takes on that task or does not. In general, it is immaterial to the institution. Faculty scholarship may enhance the prestige of the individual and the institution, but it is not required or expected.

In this atmosphere, is the climate for scholarship changing? Many feel the newly expanded definition of scholarship will serve to encourage faculty participation. In fact, an identifiable trend in community colleges is to place more emphasis on scholarship. This results in part from increased emphasis on assessment and accountability, and in part from renewed faculty interest in scholarship. Some administrators feel an increase in scholarly activities will naturally follow from the current emphasis on how teachers teach and how learners learn. The climate or scholarship at the community college might best be described by that well-worked phrase: cautiously optimistic.

ADMINISTRATION AND SCHOLARSHIP

If faculty involvement in scholarly activities is not presently influenced by institutional culture or administrative leadership, perhaps the future direction might be predicted by how administrators view their own responsibility to their professions and by the extent to which they are involved in scholarship. Here community college instructional administrators feel some of the same frustration as community college faculty: the press of time, the demands of the job, the lack of time to reflect, the sapping of creativity by leadership and management, and teaching. All those I spoke with indicated a responsibility to their profession, whether to a subject area they felt they had left behind by entering administration, or to a new field they had entered through administration: education and community colleges. All expressed regret, even guilt that they no longer "gave back" to their fields. One commented ruefully, "I've done nothing scholarly in the last two years — unless cutting budgets is scholarly!" One said, "I'm not a biologist anymore." Another biologist was struggling to remain so by teaching a class in environmental science once a year and trying to keep up with the literature, giving the impression this was a strongly felt need but a losing battle. Others commented about the writing and presentations they do as part of their job, whether within the institution or to outside groups. As one administrator pursued this thought he commented, almost to himself, "but collecting statistics is not scholarship." Another, thinking of his profession as community college education, commented, "With almost 30 years, I should have something to give back."

Community college administrators, like the faculties they come from, feel a commitment to scholarship. And, like many faculty members, they have not figured out a way to make scholarship part of their lives. They do see such activity as important and are likely to encourage and support scholarship on the part of faculty.

Support in the form of financial recognition, as a criteria for promotion or similar rewards, may not always be within the realm of the administrator or even the boards of trustees. Where faculty unions exist, rewards for scholarship may be seen as work-related issues subject to negotiations. Much may depend on how the bargaining unit and its leadership views scholarship, whether as an important faculty activity demanding recognition and support, or as extra duties added on by management.

Some administrators in nonunion situations seemed to feel they had more opportunity to reward scholarship; others in union situations felt they were restricted. Some felt the union contract under which they operated had no impact either way.

CREATING A CLIMATE FOR SCHOLARSHIP

The case for scholarship as a part of the community college mission has been strongly advanced. Proponents include educational leaders, community college faculty, and administrators. The goal has been established; how will it be met? What can those who support the goal do to create an atmosphere, policies, and an institutional climate where scholarship can happen?

The task is not the responsibility of one group; nor can any one group make the changes necessary for scholarship to happen in an institution. Following are some suggestions that may enhance and encourage scholarship.

Budget for Faculty Research

Determine guidelines and goals for the research (this may be done yearly) and issue requests for proposals to the faculty. Develop a committee of peers to review proposals and recommend grants. Eliminate proposals that request funds for normal tasks of the faculty (revising course materials and so forth). When possible, use this fund as seed money for faculty members to prepare fully developed proposals for major grants from outside agencies. Do not always expect major outcomes from a faculty member's research, but do include an evaluation component to establish the credibility of the work and to teach faculty members the importance of a strong evaluation component as they move to external grants. Here the process of engaging in research may be as important as its results.

Obtain Funding for Faculty Research

Chances are, institutions will find it difficult to fund faculty research over instructional materials, equipment needs, or staff positions. Initially, individual faculty members may find it difficult to seek funding. If the institution can draw funds from local service groups or industry, those funds can help faculty get started in research. Projects do not have to be highly esoteric; pragmatic approaches — helping the funder solve a problem — can also help faculty members solve the problem of identifying research projects and obtaining the funding to support it.

Develop Cooperative Research Ventures

Cooperative efforts, one hopes, will strengthen the funding proposal and enhance relationships among institutions. The university does not always need to be the principal investigator. Project work need not be limited to the faculty; students from both the university and the community college can participate in data gathering, manipulation, and evaluation.

Establish Endowed Chairs

There is no good reason that endowed chairs should be the purview of the university only. An endowed chair, or even a portion of one, can be established with minimum funding and give the faculty member who occupies it the time to participate in scholarly activities. This could be especially useful in the visual and performing arts. Still another advantage of endowed chairs is that neither the faculty member nor the administrator would be held to institutional workload policies, thus buying time for the faculty member. The prestige associated with endowed chairs in universities would also be bestowed to those in community colleges.

Associated with this idea could be funding for artists and scholars in residence. The opportunity to observe and work with someone actively engaged in a profession could inspire and give direction to community college faculty and students. Funding for endowed chairs and artists and scholars in residence could well be accomplished through an institution's foundation. Once associated only with private universities and colleges, foundations are now present in most community colleges. By tying requests in support of endowed chairs or artists and scholars in residence to scholarly activity and institutional quality, the institution can address the concerns of their communities and appeal to local pride.

Hold Seminars on Campus

Experts from outside the institution are not always necessary. Recognize the scholarship currently within the college. A series of seminars, held over the year, in which faculty members present their research to their colleagues can recognize successful scholarship and give ideas and incentives to other faculty members. Seminar topics might include research within a subject area, scholarship related to the teaching and learning process, or reviews of current literature and trends in the fields of teaching and learning or community college education.

Develop Exchange Seminars between Institutions

These institutions can be either other two-year colleges or four-year colleges and universities. New ideas will be introduced by those outside the institution. Recognition and encouragement will be given to those faculty members within the institution chosen to present at the other colleges. Needless to say, other benefits will spin off from such activity.

Again, both of the two preceding activities can enhance significantly the institutional atmosphere for scholarship. Neither needs to cost new dollars.

Make Presentations

Most community colleges open each new academic year with professional development or in-service days. Sometimes a nationally known educator is brought in as keynote speaker. Usually, the president and academic dean use the occasion to comment on the state of the college and to set forth goals for the year. Why not make the keynote presentation, which is given more attention than even the president's, a scholarly paper presented by an outstanding faculty member? In many institutions of higher education there is some form of recognition with perhaps a stipend attached, presented each year to an outstanding faculty member. Gear this award to the recognition of an outstanding teacher or scholar and, as part of the recognition of that award, have that individual present a lecture to the faculty and staff. This could be at the beginning of the year or sometimes during the year. The accouterments of reception, local and education press coverage should be part of the event.

Encourage Recognition of Scholarship

As an important responsibility of the professoriate, scholarship should be included as part of a faculty member's job description in the collective bargaining contract. Recognition for scholarly activities should be part of the institution's reward system. The faculty must take the lead in seeing that this measure of quality within higher education is extended to community colleges. Without faculty involvement in developing this, scholarship will remain peripheral, a sometime thing. Without scholarship as an integral part of the mission, community colleges run the continued risk of being seen as almost, but not quite, higher education.

Encourage Faculty/Student Research Projects

Every university research project relies not only on the faculty scholar but also on the student associate. The opportunity to learn scholarly methods, to work in association with an expert in the field, is an important part of university education. Why should this joy be limited to graduate students? Community college faculty members working on identified projects could well have student associates. When results are presented back to those in the field, whether through publication or through lectures or seminars, the student should, of course, be an equal colleague in the presentation. This can present a rare chance for community college students who might not otherwise have such an opportunity in their academic careers; for others who continue on to graduate work, it will have provided invaluable experience. For faculty it provides the help needed to pursue scholarly activities and is a powerful teaching vehicle.

Reward Scholarship

Rewards can come in many forms. Financial support and recognition is only one and too often suggests the need for new dollars. But other means are available. Enhanced travel is one; a faculty member can travel somewhere he or she might not ordinarily go, as to an important research library, for example. Even if the institution cannot provide full costs, an airplane ticket provides support and recognition. The purchase of books for use by a faculty member, even if they must remain college property, can support scholarly activities. Providing equipment or instructional and research materials is another reward institutions can give. This can be accomplished within the existing institutional budget and has the additional advantage of not being a part of the faculty member's salary or subject to institutional requirements.

CONCLUSION

Community colleges should support scholarship as part of the expected activity of the faculty. Scholarship can take many forms, and community colleges should encourage and recognize diverse kinds of activities. In the form of classroom research, scholarship can support assessment, accountability, and quality. In other forms scholarship can be invigorating to a faculty and provide professional credibility. Faculty scholarship should be rewarded through financial recognition where appropriate and possible, and through other means when dollars are not available. Community college administrators should set an example in scholarship and create an atmosphere where faculty scholarship can happen. However, the faculty must take the lead in making scholarship an integral part of its responsibility and the institution's reward system. Community college faculty scholarship recognized within the institution, the community, and the academy in general will enhance the position of community colleges and make them full partners in U.S. higher education in the coming decades.

REFERENCES

Boyer, E. L. (1987). *College: The undergraduate experience in America.* New York: Harper & Row.
Boyer, E. L. (1990). *Scholarship reconsidered: Priorities of the professoriate.* New York: Carnegie Foundation for the Advancement of Teaching.
Cahn, S. M. (Ed.). (1978). *Scholars who teach: The art of college teaching.* Chicago: Nelson-Hall Publishing.

Cross, K. P. (1990). Celebrating excellence in the classroom. In *Celebrations,* p. 4. Austin: University of Texas at Austin, National Institute for Staff on Organizational Development.

Myers, C. (1991, March 20). Washington update. *Chronicle of Higher Education, 37,* p. A. 32.

Vaughan, G. B. (1988, Spring). The path to respect. *Educational Record, 69,* 26–31.

9

Maximizing Unit and Individual Performance through More Individualized Faculty Roles

Russell W. Driver, J. R. Morris,
and William T. Henwood

As U.S. higher education moves through the final decade of the 20th century, there is an ever-increasing concern for maximizing the use of resources — financial, physical, and human. It is a concern fueled by a number of salient issues. Proper attention to those issues will have a significant effect on shaping higher education in the new century. Such issues include improving the quality of teaching and learning, re-evaluating the research function, increasing institutional effectiveness and accountability, and coping with the looming threat of serious faculty shortages. Clearly, these are interdependent issues.

Lozier and Dooris (1987) seemed uncertain of whether significant faculty shortages would exist across the board in the late 1990s, even though their research and that of others indicated the possibility. However, in a more recent report, the Association of American Universities (AAU) (1990) unequivocally concluded that the shortage will become a reality unless something is done to prevent or offset it. As we rapidly approach a time of anticipated faculty shortages nationwide, simple supply-and-demand economics tells us that the human resource — the now and future professoriate — will become increasingly valuable.

The AAU study proposes significant federal government assistance now in order to minimize the anticipated shortages. However, there are no present indicators of a forthcoming national program of large-scale proactive measures that will help alleviate the shortage. Therefore, universities or state systems likely will be left to their own resourcefulness.

Exacerbating the faculty shortage is an expected increase in the college-age (18–22 years old) population. According to the U.S. Bureau of the Census (1984) the nation is currently experiencing a decline in the college age population, but by the middle to late 1990s a long-term increase is expected to begin and continue until at least 2010. Additionally, El-Khawas (1990) has pointed out that the temporary decline in enrollment will be more than offset by increasing enrollments of older students and minorities and an anticipated increase in the percentage of high school graduates going to college.

If the demand for faculty far exceeds supply, as the foregoing discussion indicates, the problem of recruiting and retaining faculty will become increasingly critical in the preservation of institutional quality. Institutions must find ways to prevent quality faculty from succumbing to the lure of significant salary increases at other schools or in other sectors of the economy. Engineering and business schools already know too well the required premiums paid when hiring replacement faculty at higher salaries than had been paid. For example, in academic year 1989–90 the American Assembly of Collegiate Schools of Business (AACSB) estimated a 16 percent salary premium for new hires.

The supply-and-demand imbalances also cause problems of salary compression and inversion, which have serious morale consequences and increasingly jeopardize faculty retention efforts. As faculty leave and others are hired at premium salaries, the effect on overall faculty morale and performance becomes a very real concern.

Funding is always a significant issue in higher education, even though there are certain years when it is more of an issue in a given state. In 1990–91, for instance, there were massive cuts in funding for higher education in many states (for example, Virginia and Tennessee). Thus, it is imperative for those states to get more "bang for the buck" from their resources. Or perhaps more accurately stated, they should get more (or at least no less) bang for fewer bucks.

This chapter does not suggest that by maximizing faculty performance one can solve serious understaffing problems, which are often a reflection of business cycles and thus fluctuate by academic areas. Rather, it suggests that the use of proper systems with regard to faculty performance, evaluation, and rewards will help alleviate many of the problems associated with such debilitating issues as acute faculty shortages, high faculty mobility, and inadequate funding for higher education.

The central point of this chapter is that, by practicing sound policies with regard to the use of faculty resources, both performance and morale may be served while also providing for better use of financial resources. We advocate a system of more individualized faculty roles that takes maximum advantage of individual faculty strengths in order to raise the total performance of the academic unit.

The reader will notice that most of the rest of this chapter uses as a foundation for the discussion those institutions where research and publications are seen as components of faculty performance. It is important to note that this is a different set of schools from the "research universities," as that term traditionally is used. We recognize that there are many institutions that do not require research as a component of faculty performance, but the concepts illustrated using research can, with a little creativity on the part of the reader, be generalized to most other academic environments. For example, one could think of performance components as teaching, committee service within the academic unit, and service external to the academic unit, rather than teaching, research, and service. We chose to focus on schools that require research and publications because we believe they are among those that could benefit most from our suggestions.

WHAT THE FACULTY DOES

The enhancement of faculty performance begins with a realistic understanding of what faculty members actually do. While teaching, research, and service are the traditional roles, the available studies of faculty performance often report surprising results. Especially within the research university, but increasingly in other universities and colleges, faculty members are expected to spend a significant amount of time and effort expanding the frontiers of knowledge through published research or other such activities that often seem to be disassociated from teaching and service. In reality, comparatively few even in research universities (much less in others) actually do spend significant time on such activities.

Clark (1987), reporting on research conducted from 1983 to 1985, stated that the greatest paradox of academic work in the modern United States is that most professors spend most of their time teaching, but teaching is not the activity most rewarded or valued in higher education. Administrators praise teaching but most often reward research. Thirty years ago Caplow and McGee wrote: "It is neither an over-generalization nor an oversimplification to state that in the faculties of major institutions in the United States today, the evaluation of performance is based almost exclusively on publication of scholarly books or articles in professional journals as evidence of research activity" (1961, p. 83).

Emphasizing the same points, Willie and Stecklein (1982), in their study of faculty in Minnesota's four-year institutions, report that while faculties feel pressure to publish or perish, they spend 60 percent of their time on teaching and related activities (that is, grading, preparing, advising, and so forth) and only 5.3 percent on research and activities leading to publication. Even at the University of Minnesota, the top research university in the study, time devoted to research activities occupied only 20 percent of faculty members' time. These conclusions are consistent with those from an earlier national study that concludes, "American academics constitute a teaching profession, not a scholarly one" (Ladd & Lipsett, 1975, p. 11). The majority "teach a lot and publish little" (Ladd & Lipsett, p. 2).

There is a discontinuity present in this issue, so much so that one might even question some of the previously cited statistics. What we know about human behavior would lead us to believe that people concentrate time, effort, and results where rewards are greatest. In many — maybe most — institutions teaching is a necessary but not sufficient condition for extrinsic rewards such as salary increases, promotion, and tenure. Thus, the mere presence of teaching often will not in itself bring rewards. However, the mere presence of published research, or sometimes even the effort applied to research (almost regardless of the outcome), will bring rewards if there is a mere presence of teaching. In many schools the absence of research will prevent attainment of extrinsic rewards, but even without teaching many institutions will provide rewards as long as there is a presence of research. There is a discordant relationship between the value to the organization (in terms of extrinsic rewards) of the results of teaching and research and the actual activities occupying the time of faculty members. We believe it is critical to the enhancement of faculty performance that attention be given to this problem.

Clark's (1987) penetrating study of the professoriate in the United States emphasizes the importance of hierarchies throughout higher education. There is a hierarchy of institutions, with the research university at the apex, and there is a widespread tendency for institutions to emulate the research university and aspire to its prestige. There is a hierarchy of faculty rank, with the full professor at the top and the entry-level assistant professor at the bottom. There is a hierarchy of faculty roles, with the research role most often at the top and the service role most often at the bottom. And there is a hierarchy of disciplines, with the hard sciences at the top and the soft fields like sociology and education at the bottom. All of these represent entrenched values that frequently direct institutional policy and drive evaluation systems. They are reflected in the establishment of priorities for resource allocation and criteria for academic and monetary rewards.

As the work of Centra (1980) has demonstrated, there is wide variation among types of institutions with regard to the weights given various faculty performance roles. Research universities put the strongest weight on quality of publications, while other doctorate-granting institutions, two-year colleges, and liberal arts colleges give more weight to classroom teaching. Service activities generally are considered minor factors and at the bottom of the hierarchy.

Under the onslaught of public criticism that undergraduate education is too often ignored or given too little attention within the universities requiring research, those institutions have begun to give more attention to improving the quality of undergraduate programs. Unfortunately, they have not taken the final step. They have moved to revitalize general education, instituting more teaching awards, encouraging or requiring senior faculty to teach lower-division courses, and implementing assessment programs to demonstrate that students have learned something. Yet, with all that attention, there have been few fundamental changes in the way those activities have been rewarded.

What Boyer (1990) has called the "Berkeley Model" is still the paradigm that has commanding influence. Institutional prestige necessitates research, publication, and the getting of grants as the sine qua non of the research university. Many colleges without a primary research mission often emphasize scholarly activities leading to publications by faculty members as a way of improving institutional prestige and stature. It also must be said that many public institutions are expected to generate a significant portion of their revenues from externally sponsored research projects, regardless of how well equipped they might be for that activity. This model can be effective, but there are so many faculty members who are not actively engaged in research and who are not going to acquire grants, that better balance is needed.

INDIVIDUAL FACULTY ROLES TO MAXIMIZE PERFORMANCE

Although there is growing agreement throughout higher education that priorities ought to change, there does not appear to be a consensus on how they should change. What is required to increase overall faculty performance, enhance the quality of teaching and service, and improve the research effort? It appears there is an emerging willingness to rethink traditional faculty roles as well as traditional organizational arrangements.

Some feel the definition of research is too restrictive and rigid. Boyer (1991), in calling for a broader definition of scholarship, criticizes higher education on the basis of its rather narrow definition of research. In *Scholarship Reconsidered,* the recently released study of the Carnegie Foundation for the Advancement of Teaching, Boyer writes:

The richness of faculty talent should be celebrated, not restricted. Only as the distinctiveness of each professor is affirmed will the potential of scholarship be fully realized. Surely, American higher education is imaginative and creative enough to support and reward not only those scholars uniquely gifted in research but also those who excel in the integration and application of knowledge, as well as those especially adept in the scholarship of teaching. Such a mosaic of talent, if acknowledged, would bring renewed vitality to higher learning and the nation (p. 27).

Boyer cites the work of Richard I. Miller, whose unpublished survey of academic vice presidents and deans at 800 colleges and universities found "overwhelming support" for broadening the concept of scholarship to include more than simply research. For example, in the more limited understanding that makes scholarship synonymous with research, a textbook of surpassing quality is often regarded as an inferior contribution to an article published in a refereed journal. Boyer suggests that teaching would be enhanced by placing greater value on scholarship that adds cohesiveness and integrates knowledge. Recent moves by the AACSB to redefine as intellectual activity what previously had been operationalized as research and publications are consistent with this position. Boyer and the AACSB infer that the reward system must be changed to recognize properly the importance of scholarship related to teaching.

Appealing for greater flexibility in the assignment of faculty roles and in the evaluation system does not undermine the importance of a commitment to scholarship. It does, however, draw a distinction between scholarship and the compulsion to publish. Every institution has the right to expect that its faculty will be composed of first-rate scholars, knowledgeable and up-to-date in their fields. To quote Boyer once more, "As a scholarly enterprise, teaching begins with what the teacher knows. Those who teach must, above all, be well informed . . . steeped in the knowledge of their fields . . . widely read . . . intellectually engaged" (1991, p. 23). Miller (1972) made this point some years ago, asserting that scholarship is "a state of mind," a much broader concept than research that includes mastery of content, an inquiring attitude, a dispassionate examination of evidence, a passion for accuracy, and an openness to new ideas.

There are ways of demonstrating these qualities other than through published research, the purpose of which is to report the development or discovery of new knowledge. Some scholars are adept at discovering knowledge; others are more adept at consuming knowledge — organizing, integrating, and transmitting it. Both types of scholars can be productive in ways that contribute significantly to institutional goals.

The reward system should derive from institutional priorities and give direction and substance to faculty performance. Therefore, if institutions desire to maximize faculty performance in pursuit of the various missions of the university, it is important that performance evaluation systems and rewards encourage faculty to perform as well as possible in the particular ways they can best assist in accomplishing the multiple missions of their academic unit and the university (that is, play to their strengths).

While it might be of great importance for academic programs to maintain a reputation for excellence in scholarly research and publications, it is not essential that all faculty members contribute to those activities to the same extent. Realistically, in order for academic units or institutions to accomplish their multiple missions with limited resources, there must be an effective balance achieved in teaching, research, and service that culminates in better performance by the academic unit across all components. In the best of all possible circumstances, each faculty member would make an optimal contribution to each, and the mission of the unit would be carried out fully and happily. What is more realistic is that wide diversity exists among faculty members and, over a long career, within one faculty member. This is illustrated in the following examples:

Some faculty members are productive researchers and good teachers, and provide useful professional and institutional services. They do everything well.

Some faculty members do well in only two of the three areas of faculty responsibilities (for example, good teachers who provide useful services, but who are not productive researchers).

Some faculty members do well in only one area, but they do extraordinarily well at that activity. There are great teachers who are well read and stay at the forefront of their discipline's literature, but who are not productive researchers according to the normally accepted definition, and who avoid service activities.

At different times in their careers, faculty members may make different kinds of contributions. Those who are productive researchers early in their careers may not remain productive researchers in their later careers.

Unfortunately, some faculty members' performance may be minimally acceptable or unacceptable in all these areas. Professional development for these may be the greatest challenge of all.

Assuming the above examples to be a fair picture of faculty performance diversity, it is obvious that faculty members are going to contribute differentially to the missions of their departments and institutions. The reality of such diversity must be acknowledged and translated into effective policies and practices in order to capitalize on the strengths of individual faculty.

Research and teaching generally have different aims and require different approaches, talents, and interests. If one faculty member is best suited to teaching and another to research, then the department may be best served by promoting such specialization and adjusting the evaluation and reward systems to properly address such contributions. While there is some obvious limit to individually tailored roles during the probationary phase of one's career, when establishing scholarship and developing teaching skills are critical to long-term career goals, many tenured professors might very well be more productive and contribute more to the overall mission of their institutions by focusing their activities on the role they can and are willing to do best.

INDIVIDUALIZED FACULTY ROLES: THE CONCEPT

It is not an uncommon approach in higher education to evaluate faculty on the basis of a weighted system, assigning various weights for teaching, research, and service. How much flexibility exists in assigning weights to individual members varies considerably among types of institutions and among departments within a single institution. There is a widespread tendency to insist on some level of research effort, defined in terms of publications. For example, each faculty member might have a weighting of at least 20 percent in research, with the remainder divided between research and service. So, if a faculty member has not published in years, his or her evaluation often is still based upon the expectation that some part of the total performance will include published research. This applies particularly, but nowhere near exclusively, to doctorate-granting institutions.

The absence of flexibility with regard to the research component often has restricted rewards in other areas. Present higher education mythology is that if you give rewards to faculty members who do research and publish and deny rewards to those who do not, nonresearchers may be encouraged to become researchers, and researchers (who are presumed most able to leave for more pay elsewhere) are more likely to be retained. There is an abundance of evidence that tells us it does not happen that way. Additionally, equity theory predicts it would not (for example, Adams, 1963, 1965).

More likely, the faculty member who is not publishing, or is doing so at lower levels of quality or quantity, feels unfairly treated and unappreciated for what he or she does well. Additionally, there is even likely to be a disincentive to perform well in ways other than publishing, and physical or psychological withdrawal seems to occur all too often. As a consequence, individual and unit performance and morale can suffer. As Centra (1980) points out, faculty evaluations generally are not received well by faculty. There is a feeling that the evaluations will not be fair, will not reflect the true quality of the contributions, and — in the absence of impressive research performance — will lead to diminished rewards. All of that is the stuff of which low morale and diminished individual and overall unit performance are made.

Many institutions still employ, at least theoretically, the 12-hour teaching load as the criterion for full-time effort. (This and higher teaching loads are certainly not unusual in baccalaureate and two-year institutions.) However, in most disciplines within universities requiring research, such a teaching load takes on almost punitive proportions; indeed it is often used as an administrative response to a faculty member's lack of publications. It also relegates the faculty member to a low position in the departmental hierarchy from which ascension, within the prevailing reward system, becomes close to impossible (Clark, 1987).

Boyer (1990) admonishes higher education to accept the teacher as a valued faculty member and encourage the development of scholarship related to the teaching process. Scholarship need not always expand the frontiers of knowledge; if it enhances the transmission of knowledge — for students and for peers — it is a useful contribution. If it integrates the increasingly fragmented state of knowledge in many areas, it serves a high academic purpose.

We believe that institutions profit when most faculty members are permitted and encouraged to devote their major efforts to what they do best, so long as it serves at least one of the primary missions for which the institution exists. Reward and evaluation systems at the departmental level should be individualized as much as possible, consistent with the needs, standards, and directions of the academic unit. While disciplines differ greatly across the sciences, arts, humanities, and professional schools, institutional policies frequent-ly ignore these differences and too severely limit departmentally tailored evaluations, let alone individually tailored evaluations.

We advocate that, within the limitations of the academic unit missions, highly individualized job descriptions or contractual arrangements be entered into between the department and the individual. These should spell out the specific responsibilities on which the individual will be evaluated. Clearly our thinking on this issue assumes that, if there is a union representing the faculty, the contract allows a system of the sort we advocate. Currently it is not unusual for a faculty member to be relieved of some teaching responsibilities for a semester to concentrate on research; it is far less frequent that one would be relieved of research responsibilities to concentrate on teaching or professional service.

This is not to suggest that research should be deemphasized. Rather it is to say — as President Donald Kennedy of Stanford recently observed — we need to restore balance to the various areas of faculty responsibility and broaden our definition of scholarly activity ("Stanford Unveils," 1991). We need to be realistic in our expectations and responsibilities to the total mission of the institution.

INDIVIDUAL FACULTY ROLES: THE SPECIFICS

There are widely recognized multiple purposes to all performance evaluations (see any basic human resource management text, for example, Milkovich & Boudreau, 1988), and those of faculty are no different. One purpose of performance evaluations for faculty is to furnish colleagues and administrators with the information needed to make personnel decisions concerning retention, salary increases, promotion, and tenure. Another is to provide faculty members with useful feedback for improving performance and developing professionally.

If faculty evaluation programs are taken seriously and carried out judiciously, they should assist faculty members in strengthening their performance. Faculty evaluation and faculty development go hand in hand. Flexibility in reassigning, redirecting, or even retraining faculty members for new roles that are useful and appealing to them and their units often enhances the contributions to the overall mission of the unit of otherwise marginal contributors. Sabbatical leaves, leaves without pay, and even subsidized educational experiences are all part of this faculty development.

A successful component of any evaluation program is communication with faculty members about exactly what is expected of them and how they will be evaluated (Tucker, 1984). Explicit criteria and standards should be included in the faculty member's written assignment of activities. Having clearly defined criteria and limiting evaluations to definitively spelled out matters promotes a sense of integrity, fairness, and understanding within the faculty. However, there also should be some room for opportunistic, entrepreneurial activity so that faculty members can be even better able to contribute in a meaningful way. Whenever individual faculty members are full participants in deciding what the contract will contain, they become in a sense agents of their own destiny. From the standpoint of morale and performance, the possibilities are optimized. The give-and-take approach that personalizes the process of developing faculty assignments and sets the basis for future evaluations conveys to faculty members that they are respected officers of the university whose views are heard and whose role is appreciated.

Since evaluation is carried out largely by peers — at least at the initial stages — it is essential that the entire faculty within a unit understand and honor the formal assignment and the values or weights given to the components for evaluation. It is a legally binding contract, but, even more important for morale and performance, it is the institutional affirmation that the quality of an individual's contribution to a given performance component is not different from the quality of some other component.

There must be a clear linkage between the evaluation of assigned performance roles and rewards — both academic and monetary. This linkage and all of the details of evaluation must be spelled out in policy approved at the highest administrative levels. It is important for each faculty member to know that officially approved policies allow for different weights for different faculty members where the components for evaluation are concerned, and that the evaluation of performance based on these weights will be the basis of salary increases.

Acquiring resources for annual faculty salary increases is typically the highest priority in every budget year. One hopes that in dealing with a highly competitive marketplace, both market adjustments and merit increases can be used as proper rewards to retain and encourage faculty. In the long run there is probably no substitute for appropriate salaries. However, what often seems to be as important as the size of the salary increase is the faculty member's perception that the increase was fairly and accurately determined and an equitable share of the total rewards.

With regard to the primary missions of teaching and research, the assumption made here is that they are indeed of equal importance at the level of the department. If, during a particular year, one faculty member spends full time teaching and another spends full time on research, the unit is as well served as if the two were spending half the time in each of the performance areas. If the faculty members involved prefer to contribute in that way, then everyone is well served. If they are evaluated as having carried out their assigned roles with equal quality, they should be rewarded equally.

The example below should serve to make some of our points more concrete. This evaluation is based on a seven-point rating scale for the three most common areas of faculty performance. The areas are weighted in percentage terms, and each weight is multiplied by the rating.

Faculty member A:
    Teaching — 70% x rating of 6 = 420
    Research — 20% x rating of 4 = 80
    Service — 10% x rating of 5 = 50
                    Total points = 550

Faculty member B:
    Teaching — 20% x rating of 4 = 80
    Research — 70% x rating of 6 = 420
    Service — 10% x rating of 5 = 50
                    Total points = 550

As can be seen by the total points for faculty members A and B, they have been evaluated as making an equal contribution overall. That B did very well in research does not mean preferential status over A, whose contribution was greater in teaching and minimal in research. If policy decrees that teaching and research are equally important, the reward system must acknowledge these as contributions of equal merit and value.

Policies, of course, govern such matters as tenure and promotion, and with the current emphasis on research as a critical variable in tenure decisions at many schools, faculty member A would be disadvantaged by this evaluation. Currently there is concern that some excellent young teachers are being denied tenure because they lack a sufficient research record ("Stanford Unveils," 1991).

PROBLEMS WITH INDIVIDUALIZED FACULTY ROLES

There are, of course, several problems with an approach that individualizes job descriptions. First, it may not work well for tenure-track, but as yet untenured, faculty members who must meet the traditional criteria for tenure. Of course these criteria include significant publications. In the absence of significant changes in those criteria — and there seems to be little support for such changes within universities requiring research — the untenured faculty member is not well served by less emphasis on scholarship and publication. If institutions requiring research are to have identity and purpose different from other types of educational institutions, such reluctance to change tenure criteria in ways that de-emphasize the research role makes sense. However, the tenured associate or full professor who is not as actively engaged in research and publishing, or who wishes to focus on other areas for a time, can be best served and can serve best by devoting his or her full energies to other important responsibilities (for example, teaching, service, advising, and administrative tasks).

Another problem difficult to escape is that departmental responsibilities frequently stretch thin available resources, including faculty. Certain jobs must be done. In order to meet the array of demands, chairs often have limited flexibility. This very well may mean that faculty members must at times accept tasks they would not choose; however, in a climate that respects individuality and fosters equitable treatment, there is more likely to be a willingness to share unwanted jobs. In particular, when a faculty member is participating in the development of an annual performance plan, such assignments can be agreed to in the light of overall responsibilities. Warm and trusting collegiality within a department is the best solution to such problems. As Clark (1987) observed, if one feels fulfilled in academic work then one transcends self-interest: "One is linked to fellow workers and to a version of a larger common good. It has moral content, contributing to civic virtue" (p. 274).

The more difficult aspect of this individualized approach involves the change in attitudes that will make the contributions of the nonresearcher not only well rewarded but highly regarded. The faculty member who has a light teaching load and who is a productive researcher typically commands a position of highest prestige (and often the lion's share of rewards) over the colleague assigned to teach most of the time. Many academic administrators would affirm this hierarchical situation is the way it should be and are therefore little interested in revising reward systems.

Another taxing problem is the desire at both the departmental and institutional levels to gain stature and prestige of a national character. Research is, for the most part, the mission that builds reputations, expands visibility, and gives intellectual credibility within disciplines and among institutions. Faculty reputations are probably the most commonly accepted measure of academic quality among universities. Another measure is how much externally funded research the institution has. Academic administrators get nervous when everyone is not writing research proposals, conducting research, and publishing. Therefore, policies (explicit or implicit) often work against the individual contract approach and perpetuate the myth that the reward system will motivate faculty to do research, and that faculty members who do not do research are not worthy of reward.

One additional problem deserves mention. Many in higher education would take the more cynical view that the difficulty is not in the assignment or the reward system but too often with the faculty member who does not do research, teaching, or anything else very well. What then? What is to be done with the faculty member whose overall performance does not meet expectations? If the person is untenured, most institutions have procedures that allow nonrenewal of the contract (though the chair must be willing to exercise that option). For tenured faculty there is no single good answer to that age-old problem. Faculty development programs have been one way higher education has tried to redirect, rejuvenate, and at times re-educate such faculty members, and faculty development is certainly an approach to enhancing faculty performance.

CONCLUSION

It is difficult today for one who follows the scholar-teacher model (that is, building a career on teaching and scholarship related to teaching) to survive in the university that requires research. The deeply entrenched Berkeley model has been too powerful, the drive for national prestige too strong, and the need for external funding through grants and contracts too compelling to permit the scholar-teacher model to flourish.

The present appeal is for a realistic acknowledgment that faculty members can make valuable contributions in a variety of ways. This appeal is addressed mainly to schools that require research but by no means excludes other schools. All institutions of higher education should be interested in maximizing individual and thus total unit performance, regardless of what constitutes the components of performance for a given institution. There is both room and need for different approaches and, most fundamentally, there is and has been a pervasive desire among faculties for new models (Clark, 1987). The best efforts of each faculty member can be expected only when the assigned responsibilities permit the expression of one's highest professional interests and abilities. That should not only lead to rewards that are fair and equitable but also to that personal sense of satisfaction that one's professional calling is being fulfilled.

REFERENCES

Adams, J. S. (1965). Equity in social exchange. In L. Berkowitz (Ed.), *Advances in experimental social psychology: Vol. 2* (pp. 267–99). New York: Academic Press.

Adams, J. S. (1963). Toward an understanding of inequity. *Journal of Abnormal and Social Psychology, 67,* 422–36.

Association of American Universities, Working Group on Federal Graduate Education Policy (1990, January 11). *The Ph.D. shortage: The federal role.*

Boyer, E. L. (1991). *Scholarship reconsidered: Priorities of the professoriate.* The Carnegie Foundation for the Advancement of Teaching Series. Princeton: Princeton University Press.

Boyer, E. L. (1990, April). *The new American scholar.* Keynote address to the annual meeting of the American Association of Higher Education, San Francisco.

Caplow, T., & McGee, R. J. (1961). *The academic marketplace.* New York: Science Edition.

Centra, J. A. (1980). *Determining faculty effectiveness.* San Francisco: Jossey-Bass Publishers.

Chronicle of Higher Education. (1990, April 18). P. A13 (in box).

Clark, B. R. (1987). *The academic life: Small worlds, different worlds.* Princeton: Princeton University Press.

El-Khawas, E. (1990, April). *Responding to faculty shortages.* Address to the annual meeting of the American Association of Higher Education, San Francisco.

Ladd, E. C., & Lipsett, S. M. (1975, March 15). How professors spend their time. *Chronicle of Higher Education, 9*(5), p. 2.

Lozier, G. G., & Dooris, M. J. (1987, November). *Is higher education confronting faculty shortages?* Paper presented at the meeting of the Association for the Study of Higher Education, Baltimore, MD.

Milkovich, G. T., & Boudreau, J. W. (1988). *Personal/human resource management: A diagnostic approach* (5th ed.). Plano, TX: Business Publications.

Miller, R. I. (1972). *Evaluation of faculty performance.* San Francisco: Jossey-Bass Publishers.

Stanford unveils plan designed to elevate status of teaching. (1991, March 13). *The Chronicle of Higher Education, 15,* 19.

Stanford university's president, Donald Kennedy, has joined the ranks of those who think teaching is undervalued. (1990, April 18). *The Chronicle of Higher Education, 36*(31), A13.

Tucker, A. (1984). *Chairing the academic department.* New York: Collier Macmillan.

U.S. Bureau of the Census. (1984). *Projections of the population of the United States, by age, sex, and race: 1983 to 2080.* Current Population Reports Series (Report No. 952), p. 25. Washington, DC: U.S. Government Printing Office.

Willie, R., & Stecklein, J. E. (1982). A three-decade comparison of college faculty characteristics, satisfactions, activities and attitudes. *Research in Higher Education, 16,* 81–93.

III

SERVICE AND TECHNOLOGY MANAGEMENT

10

Evolving University Research Centers: Vehicles for Technology Transfer

James T. Kenny, Sonia R. Livingston,
John G. Veres III, and Raymond B. Wells

Academic research customarily has concerned itself with expanding the knowledge base of university disciplines. Faculty members tend to steer research toward what is unknown about their disciplines. In this tradition university mathematicians or psychologists may spend large portions of their academic careers searching and researching the as-yet-undiscovered theorem or developmental model. The emphasis in academic research lies more on validating a new discovery rather than on exploring ways in which that discovery may be used. Although there is certainly a great deal of virtue to this traditional academic approach, it may well be insufficient in meeting the ever-increasing technological demands of the 21st century (Walsh, 1990).

Managing this academic research will present major challenges for university planners and administrators as higher education approaches a new century of service. The overall tempo of scientific activity and discovery has accelerated greatly over the last few decades. This will continue to be the case in a global community that has become more technology oriented and information dependent.

The U.S. university in the years ahead will be called upon to maintain its preeminence in such competitive areas as high-temperature superconductor research, supercollider development, space power systems, materials research, computational mathematics, and solid state chemistry. It will be asked to do this in the face of chronic underfunding, salary structures less competitive than those found in industry, and research facilities seen by man as outdated and inadequate. At the same time there seems to be little reason to hope that the nation's corporations will take up the slack with expanded research and development (R&D) efforts of their own. National Science Foundation (NSF) Director Erich Bloch noted that the recent increase in corporate mergers and restructurings has reduced support for R&D in a number of industries (National Science Foundation, 1989). In view of this organizational trend, we cannot expect to see substantially increased private sector expenditure during the last decade of the century. Unless universities, through the depreciation of facilities and the inability to bear the costs of equipment, lose the physical capacity to conduct research, they will continue to have a principal role in new research initiation and a continuing responsibility in shouldering its fiscal burden.

At the campus level greater pressures are being felt by research units and the administrative systems that support them to ensure the rapid transfer of innovative technologies from the university laboratory to the production line and marketplace. One of the most persistent challenges facing our nation is the maintenance of its competitive place in a rapidly expanding world economy. New models of technology transfer, promising a speedier market deployment of university-based inventions, are viewed by many in academia, government, and industry as a promising solution to the problem of market competitiveness. Research centers have the potential to play a prominent role in the linking of basic and applied research. Opportunities exist if these centers can overcome certain barriers to success.

TECHNOLOGY TRANSFER

A number of promising techniques seem to offer coherence and utility as "value-added" elements in overall university research planning. These trends and their underpinning principles are capturing the attention of the leaders of a steadily growing number of the nation's more progressive centers of learning. As illustrations of adaptive management, they are worthy of attention and consideration. One of these trends is a movement to promote the alignment of outcome-producing university research programs with trends in economic development and technology transfer.

Beginning in the 1980s, wide-scale participation in transfer systems became a viable option for research-focused universities. This was because of changes in federal patent policy, the development of new and innovative NSF programs, the relaxation of antitrust laws, and the amendment of federal tax laws. Donald R. Baldwin (1988) notes that before the 1980s, the United States did not evince much uniformity in patent policy. A wide range of measures formulated by 26 agencies did little to encourage the commercialization of products developed by universities under sponsored agreements. Prospective industrial licensees were skeptical and unwilling to invest in technologies in which federal agencies might retain a proprietary interest. The enactment of Public Law 96-517, the Patent and Trademark Amendments of 1980, proved to be a cornerstone of today's product commercialization movement.

The newly created NSF programs — industry-university cooperative research centers, engineering research centers, science and technology centers, and presidential young investigators — also have added to an expanded technology transfer. These programs have helped focus federal research allocations and spawn a number of university-business consortia. The University of Washington's Center for Process Analytical Chemistry offers such an example. The center was organized in 1984 with NSF backing in the form of a planning grant. With the support of 20 chemical company sponsors, the unit was able to develop an outstanding computer-based information network. The short-term results for this university have been an increase in center-related scientific publications and a greatly enhanced number of invention disclosures (Baldwin, 1988).

The evolution of federal tax law has also reshaped the way universities and industry are doing business. R&D tax credits have, since 1981, encouraged corporations to donate research equipment and sponsor university research. The relaxation of antitrust laws has enabled companies to undertake cooperative research ventures. Baldwin notes that in recent years California alone has seen the growth of 40 such consortia, with a number including universities as well as private firms.

TECHNOLOGY TRANSFER MODELS

Technology transfer programs tend to follow two basic models: The first is the self-standing model, that is, the creation of an office or unit on campus that develops university patent and copyright policies, administers those policies, and stimulates university-industry interactions. This stand-alone model can prove costly because it necessitates the hiring of experts in such diverse fields as patent law and market analysis. Growing in popularity is a strategy that involves some internal administrative and staff support but relies on noncampus resources to provide specialized legal and marketing services for the commercialization of university-developed technology.

Another strategy gaining currency is locating university facilities together with high-technology businesses in research park settings. This trend has, with good reason, attracted much attention over the last decade. Today no less than 115 research parks exist nationwide, providing an innovative vehicle for joint programming between campuses and corporations. Certainly this dynamic model of university-business partnership is unique and mutually beneficial.

Even as economic development and high technology are becoming important considerations in the planning of universities, so too are they prized in modern community expansion efforts. Progressive universities and the cities of which they are a part have sought affiliation with major industries in developing joint research facilities and programs. Conversely, the science-based industries with which they have allied have made the commitment to locate close to a university to secure campus-based scientific and technical expertise in their research and product development efforts.

Industrial relocation decisions are becoming increasingly reliant on a volume of national, regional, and local information that most companies simply do not have. The decision to move or not move a subsidiary into a geographical area will sometimes hinge on complex market considerations. Most companies are wary of predicating important decisions involving substantial resource allocations on the reports normally furnished by chambers of commerce, state development offices, and federal agencies. Today they are more likely to look to a university research team or teams to provide them with the detailed demographics, retail surveys, and focus group studies that assist them in such planning.

The benefits for industry in this type of university connection are significant. Corporations have been able to accelerate the process of new product development by working in close partnership with major sources of scientific talent — faculty members and graduate students. Proximity to laboratories and specialized university units has also enabled them to ensure a more rapid technology transfer. Insofar as research parks are property ventures, their potential as magnets to attract new businesses seeking a nurturing environment is great. The aggregation of science-based companies in a cooperative setting provides opportunities for tenants to share in an abundance of information on problems related to technology, production, management, and marketing.

Correspondingly, the advantages for the affiliated university are numerous. Campus-sponsored agreements (both grants and contracts) tend to increase in number and dollar value with the development of parks. Faculty and graduate students very often are challenged with new and exciting research opportunities. Outstanding scholars may be attracted to a university because of interests in specific technologies. As corporate tenants increase in number, so do undergraduate internship possibilities. An increase in donations to scholarship programs, endowed professorships, lectureships, and laboratory equipment funds may be seen as the benefactions of corporate partners add strength to the campus private giving program.

In most cases, there are increased employment opportunities for students in the local market as the high-tech tenants expand their human resource bases to meet production challenges. In fact, access to college graduates and degree programs for employees are major motivators in corporate decisions to locate operations near university campuses. The mutual benefits for the university and its allied industry are potentially enormous. However, they do not accrue automatically, and not all parks are successful. For the process to have a meaningful genesis and a sustainable value, there must be a catalyst or two. While the university ordinarily serves as advocate, science-related industry is a prime requisite for growth. One would also hope for the proximate location of a large federal research laboratory or facilities administering a series of related, long-term federal projects. Such activity stimulates campus research and attracts a critical mass of research-focused corporations to the project area.

University research parks are one effective means of bringing industry into the academic environment (Champagne, 1990). Science parks colocated with major research universities tend to emphasize the research strengths of those universities. For example, the Chicago Technology Park focuses on biomedical research in keeping with its connection to Rush-Presbyterian-St. Luke's Medical Center (Henikoff, 1990). The Northwestern University/Evanston Research Park across town leans toward more traditional business applications (Ihlanfeldt, 1990).

A second means of bringing the university to industry lies in the organization of university research centers (Veres, 1988). Research centers bring the nuts and bolts of specialized or compartmentalized academic research to the development of new technology, with an immediate economic utility for the contracting client. In turn, research conducted within the construct of the research center lends to academic research a testing ground for validating theoretical research through real world application.

APPLIED RESEARCH SUCCESS STORIES

McKenna's model of the innovation cycle (1990) illustrates where universities may seek more involvement in these technological processes (see Exhibit 10.1 below).

Innovation begins with basic research. Academic research tends to address some of this research while industrial laboratories involve themselves with research areas requiring larger budgets and technological equipment not easily afforded by universities. The applied research phase is generally instigated by large industrial companies experiencing an immediate need to further investigate the possibilities of basic research conclusions. Universities have found themselves primarily involved in the initial basic research described in McKenna's model. Unlike the research conducted in industrial

EXHIBIT 10.1
Stages of the Innovation Cycle

Phase	Who's Involved
Basic Research	Universities
	Commercial laboratories
Applied Research	Big companies
Development	Small companies
Production/Marketing	Big companies

Source: Adapted from McKenna, 1990.

laboratories, academic research is not always technology driven; such research may not lend itself easily to application. If universities are not researching areas concerned with industry's most immediate demands, then they will continue to be excluded from the applied, developmental and production, or marketing phases of the innovation cycle. As resource banks of scientists, information, and research methodology, universities must begin to find ways to include themselves throughout the entire cycle if we are to see any significant change in the status of U.S. technology and industry.

University research efforts, separate from academic departmental structures, can provide an organized response to the technological and knowledge-based demands external to the academic institution. The move from open-ended research grants toward directed research contracts propels research centers into more of a service-oriented role of expertise. Center directors must acquire the funding necessary to keep the center's doors open and yet continue to seek the kinds of research projects that will contribute to the university's instructional mission. Many times the service-oriented nature of a center project may not generate results suitable for academic research publication. At the same time, center personnel are also researchers and will often be interested in projects that may not attract large sums of external funding. The tension emerging from the desire to conduct both basic and applied research often becomes the impetus by which university research centers reconcile the technological demands of the community with the technology-producing capabilities of the university environment.

The last decade has shown a substantial increase in the number of corporate-university research partnerships in applied research, many of which have reaped large dividends for the companies involved (Ancell, 1987; Feldman, 1987; McKenna, 1990). Many universities are meeting the needs of local businesses by establishing centers such as Eastern Illinois University's Community Business Assistance Center (CBAC) (Rives & Messenger, 1987). CBAC consultants contract with local companies for training and development seminars either prepackaged by the center or customized to address areas of concern particular to the client's organization. CBAC staff also conduct business research projects as specified by clients' marketing or economic informational needs. A spin-off of this center is the university's Small Business Institute, where CBAC staff match faculty and graduate student consulting teams with small business clients seeking the expertise of a particular university discipline.

Housed at Southern Illinois University in Edwardsville, the Center for Manufacturing and Production (CAMP) generally contracts with privately owned manufacturing companies with 50 employees or less (Lazerson & Bratsch, 1987). CAMP consultants provide engineering expertise to assist clients in cooperative engineering research and development or in equipment design and implementation. CAMP also staffs the university's Technology Communication Center, which seeks to engage inventors and entrepreneurs with businesses that may be able to use new inventions or ideas in addition to faculty resources and university facilities.

The Vehicle Research Institute of Western Washington University is even more specialized in its area of university-industry partnership research (Ross & Kurtz, 1987). The institute's director developed the Viking III car, a prototype for a production auto, in conjunction with Viking Performance Company. In addition, the institute is working with Fiba Canning, Inc., of Ontario, Canada, in the conversion of engines to natural gas. The end result of the research is to run buses on the new engines.

PUBLIC SECTOR APPLICATION

If technology is having a profound impact on U.S. business, it is only natural that this impact will be felt in the public sector. For example, in the area of financial management, the investment community is pressuring governmental agencies to provide it with meaningful and accurate data concerning government operation. Financial rating services such as Moody's and Standard and Poor's require financial data to meet the Generally Accepted Accounting Procedures (GAAP). The Financial Accounting Standards Board and Governmental Accounting Standards Board have developed extensive new reporting requirements for governmental entities. The larger the bureaucratic mass, the more difficult it may be to gather and consolidate financial data from each department or agency. Failure of a state government to provide comprehensive financial data that precisely reflects the state's financial condition may result in a lower bond rating and an investor hesitancy to commit financial resources. Changes in ratings could cost state governments millions in increased interest payments. Investors, underwriters, or bonding agencies may also be reluctant to do business with a state if financial data is not reported in a manner fully comprehensible to the business community.

Financial Resource Management System

The state of Alabama, as well as many other states, felt the impact of the business community's pressure and began looking for a plan to address it. The Alabama Department of Finance evaluated its 11-year-old, cash-based financial management system. The state found it increasingly problematic to provide citizens, elected officials, directors of its various state agencies, and the investment community with more useful and timely financial data. In late 1987, the governor recommended that the Financial Resource Management System (FRMS) be updated, enhanced, and replaced as necessary. A partnership between the Alabama Department of Finance and Auburn University at Montgomery's Center for Government and Public Affairs (CGPA) evolved to accomplish this goal.

The CGPA was contracted to work alongside state officials to investigate how the state could improve its system of financial reporting. The simplest answer was to seek a comprehensive revision in the automated financial management system, but that is where the simplicity ended. A new system would have to be customized to handle the complex, high-volume transactions that a state government generates daily. The state desired a single, enterprise-level system that could be accessed by virtually all large state agencies. In addition, some departments and agencies within the state already possessed accounting software customized for their organizations and computer equipment.

Information systems technology is one of the most rapidly changing fields today. Many organizations implement complex software systems and equipment to find that they soon become technologically obsolete. The system may still have utility for the organization, but as technology advances it will become increasingly difficult to communicate with other systems or to enhance the existing system if the basic hardware is incompatible with the latest technology in information systems. The challenge became to use current technology in a system that would last long enough to recoup the state's considerable investment in staff power, software, and hardware.

The project team focused its search for an information system on economic feasibility. Investing in a new FRMS would have very little economic value for the state if the new system were unable to meet financial reporting requirements 10 years into the future. This economic focus required the project team to build relationships with those who knew what the future in information systems would look like — the research community. The CGPA encouraged the state to develop an information system that, while meeting the current financial reporting requirements, would be technologically dynamic. The state selected American Management Systems (AMS) as the principal supplier of software. AMS was committed to meeting IBM's evolving systems application architecture (SAA) standards, a matter of some concern to the state. The state had an ongoing relationship with two of four IBM research center laboratories (as opposed to product-oriented labs) based on efforts to substantially improve the management of objects or images. Objects and binary large objects will increasingly become part of information systems. Objects include images, voice data, full motion video, and other binary forms. Image management systems are becoming commonplace today, but systems are being developed that will manage all forms of objects.

Systems Application Architecture

The state of Alabama's FRMS, a true enterprise-level information system, is currently being developed to conform to SAA. This architecture centers around a common user access method, the concepts of cooperative processing, distributed relational data, a client-server computing model, an object orientation, and enterprise information systems management services. A more complete description of SAA can be obtained from IBM. The description above contains the features of SAA exploited by Alabama's FRMS.

In addition to receiving a state-of-the-art financial reporting system that is in compliance with GAAP, Alabama will find that an employee trained in one application on the system will be able to function in many of the system's various applications with only the change of a few key strokes. The partnership benefit to IBM and AMS lies in having an actual application for what was before only an applied lab setting. The CGPA becomes the mediator for assuring that the concepts and technology developed in the lab succeeds when subjected to the real pressures on a governmental agency. University research center personnel operating in this arena must not only possess a working knowledge of information systems but also — more importantly perhaps — a knowledge of the value system under which the client must operate and a realistic understanding of the limitations of budget, time constraints, and other client pressures.

The initial question one may ask of the FRMS example is: "Is this really the transfer of technology or simply the procurement of service on the client's behalf?" Two characteristics of the FRMS project clearly illustrate CGPA's project role as the facilitator of technological transfer. First, the SAA will be applied for the first time on a large scale. CGPA provides Alabama with a risk-reduced environment separate from the state's current resource reporting system in which to discover and address problems in the system. More importantly, the relationship CGPA has established with the IBM Research Center allows for additional technological advances to be considered for inclusion in the system. For example, if the research lab develops a new technology that may be added to the system structure, CGPA consultants evaluate the effectiveness the new technology may have for the client. As a result, new technology is being fed consistently into the project. Unlike other commercial information systems purchases where the buyer contracts to obtain specified equipment based largely on the equipment's proven track record, FRMS uses CGPA as a risk buffer, allowing the state to reach farther into the future of information systems.

Can the FRMS success story be replicated elsewhere? The answer seems to be yes. Auburn University at Montgomery is a small regional university of approximately 6,000 students located in the state capital. It is not the kind of major university often associated with innovative applied research efforts.

The examples cited above are but a few in a seemingly infinite range of applied research and corresponding service opportunities that await universities positioned for growth and constructive engagement with business and government. The examples also highlight an important corollary to applied research of this nature. A campus engaged in this level of work soon finds that splendid opportunities exist for the upgrading of skills of state workers in these "modernizing" areas. These professionals learn in a simulated but operationally accurate working environment. The advantages to the recipient of these research and service activities are many but may be measured principally in savings of cost and time. High-quality university services are provided in a local environment — in some cases on-site — under dependable and manageable cost-recovery contracts with a local university.

BARRIERS TO SUCCESS

Despite these and other examples of successful business-academe and government-academe partnerships, substantial barriers to technology transfer via university research centers exist. The 800-year-old university tradition itself may prove an impediment to needed changes (Walsh, 1990). Many research centers now operate under archaic policy conceptions that limit their ability to respond to the rapidly changing technological environment. Over the next few pages we shall examine three popular myths about university centers that may limit the effectiveness of the center as a vehicle for technology transfer.

Staffing

Many believe centers should be staffed almost entirely by administrative personnel. This viewpoint perceives the research center's role as that of facilitator — brokering university resources to meet clients' needs. Centers draw expertise from faculty members, eliminating the requirement for a staff of researchers of specific disciplines. Under this model, center staff members confine their activities to writing proposals, negotiating contracts, and managing projects. Faculty members function as principal investigators and research associates, while center personnel address the project's administrative details.

Some faculty members support this facilitative philosophy of the university research center since, in addition to vesting more control of the research process in the university faculty, this model enhances faculty consulting opportunities. Using the facilitative model, the principal investigator becomes paramount since the center staff lacks the in-house expertise with which to plan and execute research designs. Methodologically sound research and effective problem solving are not necessarily mutually exclusive, but there may exist a tendency for persons from academe to design projects in a more elegant and complicated fashion than demanded by the client's problem. When additional research components do not appear burdensome to the client and provide results well suited for publication, academic researchers will almost certainly include them.

University administrators may also prefer a facilitative model to one involving a larger core staff. The increased overhead associated with a larger core staff in university research centers is often unattractive to central administration. The motion of a small staff and increased faculty participation appears to offer an efficient use of university resources. Often university faculty members are compensated at a lesser rate than that paid to external consultants. The use of the university faculty in lieu of internal center staff or external consultants may seem very attractive under this scenario.

The facilitative approach is not, however, without its difficulties. Faculty members invariably must schedule research activities around their classes. Project progress may be hindered due to problems in scheduling and coordinating project activities. Juggling the schedules of teaching faculty, working staff members, and demanding clients is not an enviable task under the best of circumstances. In many cases it represents a significant obstacle to timely project completion.

Another time-related problem involves concentration of effort. The federal courts, an arena in which centers increasingly find themselves involved, often impose very specific deadlines for depositions, hearings, and trials. Sixty-hour work weeks are not uncommon when meeting the court's, or often the client's, demands. The responsibilities associated with teaching often prevent faculty members from making such substantial time commitments.

When taking both of these problems into account, the importance of establishing a solid core staff within the university center seems obvious. An effective core staff must include specialists who can answer client questions about particular problems. If, for example, the center's central mission is economic, then the staff should include individuals capable of designing econometric models and conducting economic impact studies. Without this core, research centers cannot respond to clients with any efficiency. The facilitative model simply may not work in conjunction with research projects that do not fit well into the academic rhythms of faculty.

In the future, the need to establish effective core staffs will become even more pronounced. If the present demands rapid responses to client problems, tomorrow's centers must respond yet faster. Without a core of dedicated full-time staff, the centers of the future will find themselves relegated to the sidelines, unable to cope with their communities' problems.

Funding

A second myth concerns the financing of university research centers. Adherents of conventional wisdom believe that centers should be entirely self-supported. Obviously, this is a theory near and dear to the hearts of many administrators. University officials must search continually for additional funding; every dollar not devoted to a research center is a dollar that may be used for some other good purpose. Faculty members also may find this argument appealing for much the same reason. Since the function of the typical research center is very different from that of academic departments, faculty members may question a center's salience to the overall university mission. One argument holds that if research centers engage in activities on the periphery of the university's primary mission, then these activities must pay for themselves. Some administrators are reluctant to divert funding from the core missions of teaching and scholarly research.

Attempts at total self-support create a number of problems for research centers. One is staff stability. Earlier, we addressed the need for a core staff of specialists within research centers. It is very hard to maintain such a core when salaries are totally contract dependent. When staff money is the only funding available, staffs tend to grow or shrink as contracts come and go. If modern-day units are to respond quickly to the demands of the external environment, they must possess staff members who are not fully committed to current research projects when a new one arises. An additional benefit of substantial core staff is the opportunity for individual staff development and the improvement of research methodology during periods when staff are committed less than 100 percent to project activities.

A variant of the funding myth holds that research centers, if not totally self-supporting, should operate on a break-even basis, channelling any profits into the university general fund. This position can also create problems. One such problem deals with equipment acquisition. Center directors who possess residual profits can enhance research capabilities by investing in new equipment. Data-processing equipment is but one example. No less than other organizations, research centers must keep pace with changing technology. They cannot provide the services demanded by a modern information-based society without access to available data bases. Subscription fees associated with NEXIS/ LEXIS, Dialog, and other sources of information have become a cost of doing business.

Another problem with pay-your-own-way funding is the limitations the practice imposes on choosing projects. University research centers often perform public service work, rather than contractual services. Some or all of the costs associated with this work is donated by the unit involved. If a research center's finances are structured in such a way that cost recovery on each project is essential, the center cannot provide public service for groups that are a major part of the university's constituency. A lack of flexibility may also affect the selection of paying contracts. University research centers differentiate themselves from private consulting firms in the director's ability to say no to certain clients. This is not meant as a criticism of private consulting firms, however, a tremendous advantage in working in a partially supported research center is a certain lack of extreme economic pressure.

Equity

A widely held misconception that may considerably affect a university research center is the belief that center personnel are comparable to academic personnel, at least in salary. In centers, professional researchers with terminal degrees tend to be paid comparably to individuals holding the same degrees in academic departments. This can pose several problems: First, the time demands mentioned earlier may lead center professionals to perceive an inequity in pay, particularly during those periods when they work substantially more than 40 hours per week. Another problem stems from the researcher's mission involving contract work. The consulting work taken for granted by most faculty members may constitute a conflict of interest for center staff, creating real differences in pay.

Nevertheless, perceived inequity may not pose a major motivational problem among doctorate-holding staff. Most individuals choosing a research center career understand the rules of the game. Salaries in academic units are generally high enough to prevent widespread dissatisfaction among Ph.D.s. However, professional employees with bachelor's or master's degrees may very well be both significantly underpaid and acutely aware of this fact. In the case of those holding master's degrees, the analogous job in academe is that of an instructor. Many instructors are essentially temporary employees. They are ABDs expected to move to the professional ranks, or individuals holding terminal masters not expecting tenure. As such, salaries tend to reflect their less than permanent status. Pay for center staff holding only bachelor's degrees can be a tremendous problem for center directors. There are virtually no individuals holding only bachelor's degrees working in the typical academic unit, and therefore no comparable jobs.

In many university centers the value of masters- and bachelors-level employees is perceived quite differently from the institutions' value. In the research center this group performs much of the unit's work and bears the brunt of the long working hours necessitated by deadlines. Research center directors may find themselves stripped of any meaningful salary-based rewards for masters- or bachelors-level staff. Long hours, coupled with the low status (or nonstatus) compared to their counterparts in academe, exacerbate the perceived inequity that exists in Ph.D.-level personnel.

When faced with salary-related difficulties, many center directors have focused on other methods to motivate their employees. Porter and Lawler (1968) differentiate between extrinsic rewards and intrinsic rewards — a distinction directors should understand and value. Extrinsic rewards such as salary, fringe benefits, status, and working conditions are given by the organization. Intrinsic rewards are self-administered. They include self-recognition of a job well done, satisfaction derived from the work itself, responsibility, and personal growth. Those who would animate research must use extrinsic rewards, other than salary, as devices for motivating employees. One such device is ensuring that each professional employee has the tools requisite to accomplishing job tasks. Computers, dictaphones, and other equipment can greatly assist professional employees in the performance of their duties. Even when funds are unavailable for salary increases, center budgets may well accommodate equipment purchases, dramatically improving morale. Microcomputers on staff members' desks constitute perquisites of considerable value, an extrinsic reward not subject to the vagaries of salary constraints.

Another perquisite of a sort is the working environment itself. Carpet on the floors, flat latex paint in lieu of institutional enamel on the walls, and attractive furnishings can materially affect the way employees view their work. Improving the appearance of the work environment can also enhance a center's image with clients who are more at home in the private sector than government institutions. Pleasant work surroundings are one extrinsic reward available to the research center director unable to increase salaries significantly. Of course, directors always have at their disposal the intrinsic rewards identified by Porter and Lawler (1968), but inequity in more tangible extrinsic rewards may prove difficult to overcome.

CONCLUSIONS

Can university research centers contribute to meeting the technology transfer needs of the 1990s and beyond? The success stories at Eastern Illinois, Southern Illinois, and Western Washington universities affirm the ability of such centers to provide industry with substantial technical assistance. The FRMS under development for Alabama represents a concrete example of applying the very latest in software technology to real-world governmental problems. Nor are these isolated examples. The American Association of State Colleges and Universities recently devoted an entire volume to this topic entitled *Exploring Common Ground: A Report on Business/ Academic Partnerships* (1987).

Perhaps a more salient question is: Will research centers offer a vehicle for technology transfer? The answer is less clear. Outmoded policies often stifle center efforts. What is required of universities to overcome their lack of flexibility? Ihlanfeldt (1990) has proposed redefining the boundaries of modern universities in a seven-step process:

1. Create a top-down commitment to technology transfer.
2. Evaluate university strengths in relation to other institutions within a region.
3. Determine the needs of the home state and region.
4. Assess governmental and corporate interest in funding alliances with higher education.
5. Position the university to capture government and private support.
6. Staff adequately and properly.
7. Assume responsibility for marketing university projects.

If creative changes in universities' approaches to technology transfer can be accomplished, there is virtually no limit to the part they can play in assisting industry and government. The FRMS project demonstrates the validity of university research centers in assisting the developmental phase of the innovation cycle as well as the traditional university role of basic research. Expanded opportunities in applied research and production and marketing seem assured if universities can achieve sufficient flexibility to take advantage of them.

The question then becomes: How might today's campuses prepare themselves for effective participation in tomorrow's research environment? While one cannot divine, with any degree of certainty, the new theories or investigative possibilities that will capture the imaginations of tomorrow's researchers, it is clear that today's scientists are engaged in an accelerating process of knowledge acquisition. The body of knowledge and the methodologies used to approach it are in constant flux. The process also depends upon context, that is, inquiry and investigative productivity seem to flourish in some settings and fail in others.

University planners, and research administrators in particular, must make organizational adjustments to better position their institutions and units in the intense competition for basic and applied research dollars. The development of such evolutionary strategies requires much time, commitment, and patience, and effective preparation must begin with a rigorous examination of institutional values. University leadership must first of all understand the integrative role a campus can and must play in society. The successful synthesizing and transmission of scientific data, technical information, and civilization's ethical values are the responsibility of a modern institution of higher education. In the main, enhanced self-understanding by such institutions will promote more effective and adaptive methods of research management.

University research in the future is less likely to occur in a vacuum and, in the aggregate, will most likely represent a healthy balance of basic and applied initiatives. To meet this challenge in a proactive fashion, campus leaders must precede their search for future institutional relevance with a strong assertion of institutional self-awareness. Academia must then move to capitalize on its special relationship to the known and knowable. In so doing, its constituency must seek to conduct campus affairs in an externally poised but ethical, humane, and responsible manner. In every sense it must guard its prerogative as standard-bearer of the cumulative and enlightening values of civilization. Adaptive management encourages the seeking and seizing of the abundant opportunities tomorrow may bring. However, this is best done from a historically cognizant and elevated perspective. The future vitality of research, and perhaps all of higher education, will depend upon its leaders' willingness to meet change and to act for the public good in a responsible, constructive, and convincing manner.

REFERENCES

American Association of State Colleges and Universities. (1986). *The higher education-economic development connection: Emerging roles for public colleges and universities in a changing economy.* Washington, DC: Author, pp. 10–27.

Ancell, N. S. (1987). The benefits of business/academic partnerships: A corporate perspective. In *Exploring common ground: A report on business/academic partnerships* (pp. viii–xi). Boston: Author.

Baldwin, D. R. (1988, fall). Academia's new role in technology transfer and economic development. *Research Management Review, 2*(2), 1–6.

Champagne, J. E. (1990). The role of universities in marketing research and science parks. In W. Ihlanfeldt (Moderator), *Marketing in the 1990s.* A session of the World Conference of Research and Science Parks, Chicago.

Collins, T. C., & Tillman, S. A. (1988). Global technology diffusion and the American research university. In J. T. Kenny (Ed.), *Research administration and technology transfer* (pp. 5–20). San Francisco: Jossey-Bass Publishers.

Feldman, S. (1987). The benefits of business/academic partnerships: A university perspective. In *Exploring common ground: A report on business/academic partnerships* (pp. xii–xxi). Boston: Author.

Hackman, J., & Oldham, G. (1975). Development of the job diagnostic survey. *Journal of Applied Psychology, 60,* 159–70.

Henikoff, L. (1990). In W. Ihlanfeldt (Moderator), *Marketing in the 1990s.* Welcoming remarks at a session of the World Conference of Research and Science Parks, Chicago.

Hughes, G. D. (1990). Managing high-tech product cycle. *The Executive, 4*(2), 44–55.

Ihlanfeldt, W. (1990). The role of universities in marketing research and science parks. In W. Ihlanfeldt (Moderator), *Marketing in the 1990s.* A session of the World Conference of Research and Science Parks, Chicago.

Lazerson, E. E., & Bratsch, G. (1987). Southern Illinois University at Edwardsville: Center for advance manufacturing and production. In *Exploring common ground: A report on business/academic partnerships* (pp. 114–18). Boston: Author.

McKenna, R. (1990, May). Technology marketing: It isn't what you think. In R. A. Reck (Moderator), *Marketing in the 1990s.* A session of the World Conference of Research and Science Parks, Chicago.

National Science Foundation. (1989, March). Report on selected congressional activities (NSB-89-48, p. 21). Washington, DC: Author.

Paré, T. P. (1990). Why some do it the wrong way. *Fortune 500, 121*(11), 75–76.

Porter, L. W., & Lawler, E. D. III. (1968). *Managerial attitudes and performance.* Homewood, IL: Richard D. Irwin.

Rives, S., & Messenger, A. F. (1987). Eastern Illinois University: Community business assistance center. In *Exploring common ground: A report on business/academic partnerships* (pp. 92–95). Boston: Author.

Ross, G. R., & Kurtz, S. (1987). Western Washington University: Examples of direct delivery of services. In *Exploring common ground: A report on business/academic partnerships* (pp. 123–27). Boston: Author.

Veres, J. G. (1988). Managing a modern university research center. In J. T. Kenny (Ed.), *Research administration and technology transfer* (pp. 61–72). San Francisco: Jossey-Bass Publishers.

Walsh, E. M. (1990). The changing university: A discussion of new directions including the distributed or nodal university. In E. M. Walsh (Moderator), *Marketing in the 1990s*. A session of the World Conference of Research and Science Parks, Chicago.

11

Comprehensive University Extension in the 21st Century

William I. Sauser, Jr. and Ralph S. Foster, Jr.

Most universities list, among their primary missions, extension, outreach, or public service. Regardless of the size of the institution, and no matter which term is employed, the concept is the same: application of the university's resources for the benefit of the populace. The comprehensive university's mission in extension, which is firmly interwoven into the fabric of the U.S. university system, will become even more important in the 21st century. Universities that have not already done so must begin now to plan an extension strategy for the next century. Those with a strategy in place must periodically review and revise it.

This chapter is designed to help university administrators understand and design effective strategies for comprehensive university extension in the 21st century. It begins with a description of the modern university's comprehensive mission in extension, followed by a perspective on semantics. A review of extension's historical background is followed by an analysis of the evolution of organizational and delivery structures. An outline of the strategic planning process, along with some opportunities and challenges for extension, precedes a discussion of two important issues facing university administrators: how to develop the personnel needed to administer the extension mission in the future, and how to reward extension programming. The chapter concludes with a challenge to 21st-century educational leaders.

UNDERSTANDING UNIVERSITY EXTENSION

The Mission

The modern comprehensive university's mission in extension is to apply its knowledge base to address effectively issues of concern to the people in its service area and beyond. Extension programs are designed to improve quality of life and address lifelong learning needs; enhance economic and community development; strengthen individuals, families, businesses, governments, and organizations; and implement research findings. Extension delivery methods include a variety of print, electronic, and personal means of presentation for providing useful information to people who need it.

Effective extension requires: a needs analysis to determine client demand; a program (workshop, seminar, short course) or project (demonstration, videotape, pamphlet, teleconference) tailored to meet identified needs; program or project delivery; and documentation of impact. Parallels among extension and the typical university's other two primary missions are diagrammed in Exhibit 11.1

EXHIBIT 11.1
Parallels among the Three Primary
Missions of the Typical University

	Research	Instruction	Extension
Determine a Need	Literature review and observation to determine hypotheses.	Curriculum review and analysis to determine instructional objectives.	Needs analysis to determine client demand for programs and projects.
Create a Mechanism	Devise experimental or other research methodology.	Create syllabus, course outline, instructional aids.	Design and develop a program or project tailored to address identified needs.
Implement the Mechanism	Carry out the research and collect data.	Teach the course in an effective manner.	Deliver the program (workshop, short course) or project (demonstration, videotape, pamphlet).
Evaluate the Impact	Analyze and discuss results relative to hypotheses.	Evaluate student performance relative to objectives.	Document impact in addressing identified client needs.
Document the Process	Present/publish the paper.	Collect course evaluations and credit hour information.	Prepare a summary, report CEUs, report client reactions and impact results.

All three of the university's missions involve gathering and sharing information. The primary purpose of research is to discover facts and build knowledge through systematic inquiry; this knowledge is typically shared with the research community through journal articles and paper presentations. The primary purpose of instruction is to disseminate collected knowledge in a systematic manner — typically in a classroom setting — for academic credit. The primary purpose of extension is to gather and share information that can be applied to address specific needs of a client group.

Perspective on Semantics

Attempts to use such terms as "extension," "cooperative extension," "continuing education," "lifelong learning," and "public service" synonymously among institutions have caused tremendous confusion as to the true nature of a university's outreach mission. Unfortunately, there are few universally accepted definitions among institutions; as institutions form more collaborative relationships in the future, common usage of terminology must surface.

One primary source of confusion has been the application of outreach terminology by institutions to both credit instruction for nontraditional students and to noncredit assistance, development, renewal, and enrichment programming. Extension has sometimes been used to denote degree programs that have been extended — to a setting other than the traditional campus classroom environment; to a body of students who, because of their age or work experience, do not fit the portrait of the traditional student; or to coursework provided during hours other than normal class times. Similarly, continuing education and lifelong learning have sometimes been construed to mean the availability of credit programs for the continuation of one's work toward finishing a degree or obtaining an additional one, regardless of the person's stage of life.

In the true sense of a comprehensive outreach effort, one must draw the line in terminology based on whether the activity falls more in the mode of the academic instruction mission of the institution, or that of the provision of applied resources to the public at large — the extension mission. Because of rapidly changing technology, organizations and individuals are finding it difficult to acquire ever-increasing amounts of information through the process of earning more and more formal degrees. Institutions of higher learning are, therefore, being called upon to provide immediately applicable information to individuals for the enhancement of their personal and professional lives, if for no other reason than to enable them to keep up with societal and technological changes.

In that respect, the institution must actively provide its resources on an ongoing basis (continuing education) to persons regardless of age or status in life (lifelong learning) for the enhancement of one's career (professional development), business (technical assistance), or personal life (public service). That whole, comprehensive provision of resources intended to help people keep up with their changing technological, social, and moral world is, in essence, what extension has come to mean. While the credit degree will continue to represent a level of mastery obtained through a relatively lengthy process of formal study, extension programming will be recognized as the means to keep that mastery current once the individual leaves the formal educational establishment.

EXTENSION: FROM YESTERDAY TO TOMORROW

Historical Origins

The organization, scope, and disciplinary coverage of the outreach effort are associated directly with the historical background and foundations of an institution itself. For example, cooperative extension outreach is found in land-grant agricultural institutions; technical institutes feature outreach rooted in professional continuing education; many liberal arts institutions provide general enrichment public service programming. Comprehensive university extension is a blending of these outreach methods and activities that have evolved over the past two centuries, representing a convergence of at least three main historical movements: university public lecture circuits, land-grant institutions, and the Cooperative Extension Service.

The nation's early leaders recognized the importance of extending educational opportunities to the people. In the late 1820s, towns across the country had begun to establish local adult learning centers, or "lyceums," for presentation and discussion of topics of mutual interest and for scientific presentation (Russell, 1990, p. 28). This was followed by the involvement of major universities, such as Yale, in public lecture series. While trustee of the Lowell Institute, Lawrence Lowell outlined plans for public service courses to be taught by Harvard's faculty, a spirit of public service as a function of the university that he continued to encourage after he became president of Harvard in 1909 (Russell, 1990, p. 29).

This establishment of a public service commitment in higher education was furthered by the land-grant colleges created by the Morrill Act of 1862, which were designed to extend a practical education to the common man of the industrial and agricultural classes (Caldwell, 1976). The Morrill Act was comprehensive, though, and did not exclude the teaching of classical studies, nor did it limit clientele to farmers and craftsmen; the theme of the act addresses education regarding "the several pursuits and professions in life" (Caldwell, 1976, p. 12). This concept of a professional education was reinforced by the Hatch Act of 1887, which established experimental agricultural research stations to support the land-grant institutions' instructional efforts through public demonstration techniques (Russell, 1990, p. 35).

The establishment of the Cooperative Extension Service brought the resources of the university to bear on almost every aspect of the public's personal, family, and work life. The Smith-Lever Act of 1914 created this network to disseminate agricultural and home economics information and to incorporate all extension work done in state agricultural colleges (Rasmussen, 1989, p. 50). The result was an information delivery and technical assistance system that could conceivably reach every citizen in a state.

As land-grant universities have added disciplines beyond the traditional agricultural or mechanical arts, the cooperative extension mechanism has served to facilitate the dissemination of other resources to the community, such as professional continuing education or public enrichment programs, or has served as the model to do so. As the United States has transformed from a rural society to an urban one, programming based on emerging issues instead of disciplines is causing the further evolution toward a comprehensive university outreach mission.

Organizational Issues

There are about as many models for outreach organization as there are institutions across the country. Some are organized as a subsidiary to the credit programs in the academic affairs branch of an institution, while others are housed in the research division and billed as "applied research." Others are organized as a totally separate public service division, with offerings unrelated to the institution's academic disciplines and the staff segregated from the faculty. Still others are an offshoot of the university administration as a public affairs advocate, with informational programming serving mainly to promote the image of the institution. Some institutions offer no organization for their outreach at all other than to have a central coordinator who reports on whatever outreach activities the various academic departments may elect to do.

The most definitive organizational models for outreach are found in the land-grant universities that have cooperative extension services. In these universities there exists a clear legal mandate for an organization that applies the research base of the institution, using instructive and demonstrative methods, to the direct benefit of the public. Thus, a centralized method of organization and a strong relationship exists between the on- and off-campus staffs and the faculty in the disciplines primarily related to cooperative extension. Over the years, as these institutions added other disciplines not directly related to the original focus of cooperative extension, the impetus for outreach often was not felt or was incorporated externally from the existing extension structure — an evolutionary move toward decentralization.

The natural outcome of a decentralized structure is that a university's extension programming becomes almost totally discipline based; the engineering school produces programs for engineers, the pharmacy school for pharmacists, and so on. The indications for the future, though, are decidedly away from the discipline-based programming mode to one of addressing multi-faceted societal issues. People and problems are no longer isolated by distance and communication; in the expanding age of information and communication, communities, businesses, families, and individuals share broad societal concerns that must be addressed from a variety of perspectives.

In the findings of the Futures Task Force, cooperative extension was failing to keep up with societal issues, in part because it had become too rooted in its college alliances and disciplinary orientation (Futures Task Force, 1987). The task force called for the extension organization to be driven by compelling issues, and for its resources to be marshalled from beyond traditional program boundaries to meet those issues in a proactive manner. Similarly, the futuring panel of the Cooperative Extension System called attention to society's move to a global economy and recognized that extension must use all the resources of the university (Geasler, Bottum, & Patton, 1989). The movement to an issue-based, multidisciplinary programming system has profound organizational repercussions.

Comprehensive university extension in the future will walk an organizational tightrope between centralization and decentralization in order to achieve the diversity of programming necessary to solve broad societal problems. Public pressure for societal assistance will, no doubt, cause universities to reevaluate and mobilize their outreach mechanisms. Because of funding limitations, the extension organization will never be able to duplicate the entire interdisciplinary resources of the university, nor would the university be able to stand the organizational burden of such a dual system. There is also validity to the premise that the best person to extend information about a subject is the one who actively researches and teaches in the subject area. For these reasons, extension will become more decentralized and diversified.

To achieve a comprehensive extension thrust, however, central administration must insist that all university divisions contribute to the outreach mission. The central administration must integrate the working relationships among extension, research, and instruction, rewarding effective interdepartmental collaborations (Meier, 1989). Central administration must direct the instructional curriculum and the research agenda to address the same societal issues facing extension. A central administrative source must develop information-gathering mechanisms for defining the issues. It must marshal and guide multidisciplinary resources — balancing overlapping disciplinary and professional interests — in order to have the cohesive programmatic approach needed to resolve societal issues. Centralized reporting is essential for evaluating program effectiveness.

A discussion of an issues-driven, multidisciplinary extension thrust carries with it an illusion of great institutional size. Yet, it should not be assumed that only large land-grant or state universities can sustain an effective outreach effort. Nowhere is it mandated that an institution should meet all of society's needs. Indeed, small community colleges, private institutes, and liberal arts schools can make a considerable impact on specific societal problems, either by applying their resources to address an issue that falls within their disciplinary coverage or by becoming part of a larger collaborative effort among other institutions.

For example, a private liberal arts college may make a great contribution toward combatting illiteracy in its community because of its proximity to the problem and its resources at hand. Similarly, a technical school could play a role in the economic recovery of a community by offering to provide skill updates for the local work force as part of an effort to draw new industry to the area. The size or scope of an institution may determine the direction and magnitude of its outreach thrust, but by no means should this eliminate any educational organization from fostering an extension mission.

Because of the dearth of monetary resources, extension must avoid duplication of facilities and technology. A systematic approach to resource development and sharing must be used for specialized meeting facilities, technological applications, communications, and marketing, as well as programming. In many cases, facilities and resources once designed for a single function must be adjusted for collaborative endeavors among units. Centralized budgeting of funds among the extension program thrusts is essential to promote equitable distribution of funds along issue priorities. Resource and programmatic coalitions between institutions must be negotiated between key centralized representatives rather than among dozens of individual university bodies.

The nature of issue-based programming demands interdisciplinary attention and commitment. The integration of the research, instruction, and extension functions of a university leads to a decentralized organizational pattern as far as personnel and departmental units are concerned — particularly where programmatic teams will be formed by collaboration among units that do not report to the same administrative leadership. Yet, a loose organizational confederation cannot acquire and maintain the physical and technological resources needed for a true comprehensive university extension thrust. Here, the adage that the whole is greater than the sum of its parts holds true; a well-organized, but not dictatorial, central leadership must guide and control certain aspects of the extension organization.

Modern Extension Delivery Modes

Traditionally the concept of extension has been based on a person-to-person exchange of information. People would travel to the institution, visit the extension office, and take advantage of the variety of instructional, technical, and information services available on campus. Since there were few reliable transportation alternatives in the 19th century, an institution's outreach effort was understandably focused on citizens in nearby communities.

Populations eventually grew beyond the original population centers in which many institutions of higher learning were located. Many such institutions found themselves serving an ever-decreasing share of the population they were mandated to serve. The establishment of a statewide cooperative extension service with offices in each county and population center presented institutions with the opportunity to provide outreach programming to increased numbers of people within a short distance from their homes or farms.

As demand grew for extension, institutions could no longer add enough personnel in every location to accommodate all requests for individual assistance. While personal demonstration remained the backbone of extension education, area meetings and mass distribution of printed materials became effective methods of disseminating outreach information with the limited human resources at hand (Rasmussen, 1989, p. 92). In time, extension made use of electronic technologies such as radio and television for broad program delivery.

In the 21st century, extension will continue to face the dilemma of meeting public demand for information with limited resources. Undoubtedly, as the costs of both personnel and building maintenance continue to rise, budgetary constraints on the extension organization will force the reallocation of resources to more efficient and cost-effective means of meeting client demand for information. This will lead to the ultimate reorganization of the extension's physical plant, as well as its technological structure. Examples of what we see happening follow.

Consolidated Operations

In order to avoid drastic reduction in quality programming, extension may eventually face these limitations in funding with the merging of county offices in favor of multicounty and regional operations. The drive toward regional extension centers will be facilitated by collaborative efforts among similar institutions seeking to avoid duplication in services. Such multicounty, multi-institution, and even multistate collaborations will also serve to dissolve the geographical boundaries that have often limited extension coverage (Meier, 1989). Allocation of staff and resources based on population, local funding, and area need will take the place of uniform distribution ("Staffing and Funding," 1990).

Conference Centers

Extension programming targeted to specific groups of clientele — such as professional continuing education recertification courses and business development seminars — are more cost effective when offered in sessions to groups of participants in a specialized conference site. To the degree that professions and businesses will have to cope with the ever-increasing pace of new information and change, the demand for such seminar programming undoubtedly will increase (Kirkland, 1989). This will require conference centers offering specialized presentation and demonstration technology, flexible room organization, and highly trained and responsive personnel to support the programming function.

Because of the relatively high cost of development, location will be key to the success of such a conference center (Wilderman, 1989). The center must be located close to the host institution in order to take advantage of its programming resources in the faculty, thus encouraging use by a variety of client groups. Institutions must adopt an expanded marketing thrust in order to identify and actively solicit groups that can travel to the conference center site. These client groups will be expected to pay for using the center so that the university will realize a return on its capital investment.

Computer Networks

Extension professionals currently enjoy the use of comprehensive internal information systems, as well as linkages with other institutions and agencies (Burleson et al., 1987). These systems will be expanded in the next century to allow for direct public access from any remote computer site. This will free extension professionals to perform the more critical consultations that require personal observation. These professionals will also benefit from such a system by being able to access information in the field rather than having to return to the nearest office to use the computer. One important step toward a viable public access computer information network is for extension to support industry standardization of operating systems (Ezell, 1989).

Satellite Transmission

One of the most exciting and versatile additions to extension's resources is satellite transmission and receiving capabilities. Satellites can be used to transmit not only video and audio programming, but printed material and computer information as well. A survey performed by the Public Broadcasting Elementary and Secondary School Service indicated that video programming via satellite currently surpasses all other usage (PBS Elementary/ Secondary Service, 1989). The extension organization of the future must capitalize on the satellite's full potential for information handling.

Video-based Programming

Extension will take a leadership role in the area of video programming, not only because of the large prospective audience but also the inherent travel, personnel, and time savings that satellite transmission can mean for the extension organization. A program team at the institution can deliver its presentation, incorporate visual aids and subsidiary video, and offer opportunities for live interaction to any group or individual with a receiving dish, television, and telephone. Hundreds of sites can receive the presentation simultaneously via satellite at a cost far lower than if the organization attempted the same coverage with a series of on-site presentations. With extension facing a likely future of reduced funding and scaled-down operations, satellite technology presents an opportunity for expansion, rather than reduction of programming coverage.

Field Technology

Extension professionals must continue to visit remote locations to meet the needs of individuals and groups who cannot be served at a central location or through public access technology. For instance, as the nation's population grows older, comprehensive university extension undoubtedly will move to meet the needs of those who, because of their physical limitations, must be served in or near their homes. In the past, serving groups in the field has been a time- and labor-intensive process. In the future, technological advances in computers and satellite transmission will reduce much of extension's costly movement of programming and consultative professionals to remote locations.

The agent in the field, the forester in the woods, and the consultant at the plant site will have on command the vast information resources of the university and other data bases via satellite. Armed with cellular phones and briefcase-sized satellite dishes, extension professionals will make on-site analyses of problems and critical recommendations in the field (Ezell, 1989). The wait of hours, days, or even weeks for the professional to travel from site to research base — and back again — truly will become a thing of the past.

UNIVERSITY EXTENSION OPPORTUNITIES

The changes we envision for extension in the 21st century are myriad. In order to prepare for the future, university leaders must begin immediately to create strategic plans for the university extension mission. The typical strategic planning process for colleges and universities of all sizes calls for considerable environmental scanning, as well as surveying of the citizenry and other stakeholders to determine needs and opportunities. In addition, critical analyses of the institution's strengths, weaknesses, and external challenges must be performed. Finally, considered decisions must be made regarding how the university desires to be positioned in meeting its mission and how to accomplish this positioning. The ideal process is an iterative one that includes analysis and review at all levels of the organization. The desired outcomes are a clear sense of purpose, concrete action steps to accomplish identified needs, and organizationwide commitment to the plan.

Extension Opportunities

Opportunities abound for university extension. The need is great for research-based information and assistance throughout the state, the nation, and the world. In creating strategic plans for extension at Auburn University, a number of opportunities, as described below, were identified that can, in most instances, be generalized to other settings. In fact, community colleges and small liberal arts colleges can devise very creative programs to capitalize on some of these opportunities.

Cooperative Extension

Consistent with the land-grant tradition, universities with cooperative extension services have many opportunities to serve the citizenry (Futures Task Force, 1987; Dalgaard, Brazzel, Liles, Sanderson, & Taylor-Powell, 1988). Priority areas identified by the Alabama Cooperative Extension Service (1987) include:

regain agricultural and forestry profitability with emphasis on business management skills, production systems, alternative enterprises, and marketing strategies;

develop, conserve, and manage natural resources with emphasis on water quality and quantity, soil preservation and productivity, and human and cultural uses;

enhance family and individual well-being with emphasis on family stability, wellness, diet and nutrition, resource and financial management, home food production and preservation, and homes and home grounds;

develop human resources with emphasis on leadership and volunteerism; and

revitalize rural communities with emphasis on economic viability, community services and facilities, public policy, and rural-urban relationships.

These are broad themes that encourage the creation of innovative programs, such as workshops designed to teach young adults how to manage their money, or young mothers how to prepare nutritional meals for their children. Institutions of all sizes, if committed to outreach and public service, can devise meaningful programs in the communities they serve.

Economic Development

Many universities have extensive programs of research in a variety of disciplines. By applying the results of this research through extension programs, universities can broaden and diversify the agricultural, industrial, and educational base of their states, thus furthering the economic well-being of the citizenry. The chapter by Kenny, Livingston, Veres, and Wells in this text provides excellent examples of how this can be done. Armenakis et al. (1989a) present a case example for developing a strategy for directing the university's resources toward economic development of the surrounding region.

Lifelong Learning

Citing a U.S. Department of Education report (Hill, 1987), the American Council on Education states:

> The dramatic increase in the number of people taking adult education courses between 1969 and 1984 reflects a changing concept of education in which formal study does not stop with a high school or college degree, but continues throughout adulthood. . . . Further evidence of this changing concept of education is the money adults are spending for non-degree courses. . . . In 1984 alone, participants spent $3 billion for adult education courses ("Number of Adult Ed Participants," 1987, p. 8).

Modern universities have a tremendous opportunity, through their programs in extension, to address the increasing educational demands of adult learners. Extension activities could complement innovative for-credit instructional programs designed for the special needs of these nontraditional learners (Best & Eberhard, 1990). This is a niche many community colleges are moving to fill.

Recent data indicate that two-thirds of adult education courses are taken for job-related reasons, and that there is an increase in the number of courses being taken "to meet a requirement for obtaining or renewing a license or certificate as required by law or regulation" ("Number of Adult Ed Participants," 1987, p. 8). Universities with strong professional schools and comprehensive educational programs have the opportunity to serve as major providers of professional and personal continuing education offerings.

Entrepreneurial Development

Many of the new jobs created throughout the nation are in small businesses. Unfortunately, many of the small businesses started each year fail because of undercapitalization, lack of managerial skills, or poor planning. By educating entrepreneurs and guiding them as they form new businesses, universities can assist in economic development, reduce unemployment and related social problems, and prevent the unnecessary loss of personal and venture capital. Many institutions have developed small business development centers (Chrisman, Nelson, Hoy, & Robinson, 1985) and other outreach units (Armenakis et al., 1989b) to meet this need.

Educational Excellence

The quality of public education in the United States is a major concern of many of its citizens. Universities are uniquely positioned to be a major force in increasing the competence of teachers and educational administrators through their outreach programs and by upgrading teaching skills in critical subject areas, such as sciences, mathematics, and foreign languages.

Human Resource Development

Many economically deprived citizens need literacy education, life skills training, and health and nutrition education. Furthermore, many of these citizens do not possess the means to help themselves. By directing energy and resources to address these issues, universities can exert a major influence in the continued development of the nation's human resources. Programs that could be developed by even the smallest colleges might include one-on-one literacy education programs, workshops on food selection and preparation, programs to teach basic applications of mathematics — such as making change and balancing a checkbook — and many forms of exercise, stress management, and fitness programs.

Special Needs

A number of citizens — persons with physical disabilities, mental impairments, emotional disturbances, sensory impairments, financial trouble, learning disabilities, substance addiction — have needs for exceptional care, concern, and rehabilitation. Through direct service provision in clinical settings, as well as education and training programs for service providers, universities have an opportunity to contribute to the enhanced quality of life of these citizens.

Youth at Risk

Youth are at risk throughout the nation. The National Initiative Task Force on Youth at Risk (1989) highlights as key risk factors poverty, suicide, functional illiteracy, child abuse and neglect, emotional and mental health problems, drug abuse and alcoholism, and teenage pregnancy. Modern universities are in a pivotal position to focus their considerable expertise in these and related areas and to lead community-based emphases on human capital and youth development. After-school recreational programs and efforts to involve college students in one-on-one work with youth (such as Big Brothers and Big Sisters) are outstanding examples of how any college can get involved in this important area.

Excellence in Government

Professionalism and the desire to upgrade knowledge, skills, and abilities is definitely on the rise in state and local governments (Sauser, Smith, & Salinger, 1982). Through extension, modern universities can contribute significantly to the increasing professionalization of government employees by offering technical assistance and professional development programs. The chapter in this volume by Kenny et al. provides impressive examples of how a medium-sized urban campus of a university system is making major contributions in this area. Leadership programs for local government officials can be offered by small colleges as well as big universities.

Citizenship Education

The development and presentation of creative extension programs in ethics, values, choices, social and civic awareness, cultural and historical heritage, ethnic appreciation and relations, health and nutrition, and continuing self-development are challenges for which many universities are well prepared. Examples of such programs include efforts to encourage youngsters and their grandparents to read to each other, or presentations regarding local history and culture.

Aging

"The graying of America" is a well-documented phenomenon. The life expectancy, average age, and work life of U.S. citizens are all increasing. Universities have an opportunity to focus attention on such issues as the quality of life of the elderly; renewing respect for senior citizens; aging and productivity; volunteerism, community action, and alternative postretirement activities; and tapping the wisdom and experience of older citizens. The Elderhostel model (Knowlton, 1977) has been followed successfully by many universities seeking to offer meaningful outreach programs to older adults.

Environmental Issues

Experts throughout many universities can provide leadership in such issues as solid waste management, hazardous waste disposal, air and water quality, acid rain, land use and community planning, ozone depletion, reforestation, energy conservation, and alternative energy sources. Creating multidisciplinary extension teams is crucial to addressing these issues affecting life on earth. Teaming knowledgeable professors with local community action groups can be an effective means of dealing with these critical issues in a local setting. Creating a speakers list of faculty members and their areas of expertise, then providing that list to civic clubs, professional associations, newspapers, and radio and television stations are projects any institution of higher education can adopt.

Global Dimensions

Educational, business, and governmental leaders are calling for the United States to become more sophisticated in incorporating the global dimension into its national policies. Universities with international expertise can expand extension activities beyond state or national borders. By focusing attention on international economic competitiveness, cooperative ventures, and world affairs, the modern university can provide increased leadership in global development.

Challenges to Extension

Along with the exciting opportunities for extension mentioned above, the external environment poses some challenges to the extension mission of many universities. The implications of some of these important external challenges are discussed below.

Funding Limitations

Most universities have a limited funding base at present and few prospects for dramatic funding increases in the foreseeable future. This means they must prioritize their extension activities and seek to gain the greatest benefit from available funds. Universities must also be innovative and flexible in seeking and using external funds. Private donor support, contractual and grant support, and user fees must be aggressively pursued and obtained to supplement local, state, and federal budgeted funds for extension.

Accountability Demands

Recent years have seen an increased demand from government accrediting bodies — and the public at large — for accountability from state-supported universities. This demand must be met with positive, decisive action. The university must be in a position to document, for example, progress in meeting affirmative action, equal employment, and equal-opportunity educational policies, procedures, and goals. The university must also be prepared to show how public funds allocated for extension have been used for the betterment of all the citizenry. It is incumbent, therefore, to establish and maintain records of extension programs and their impact. Decisions regarding the distribution of extension-related funds must be based on projections and anticipated measures of positive impact.

Private Sector Competition

The increased demand for continuing education courses has not gone unnoticed by the private sector. As a result, numerous for-profit education and training institutes have been formed, and many professional associations and large business organizations have created their own internal educational facilities. S. T. Hill states:

> Non-school providers of adult education became more important from 1969 to 1984, increasing their share from 37 percent to 47 percent. . . . One type of provider — business and industry — grew to such an extent that they almost equaled 4-year colleges and universities in the number of adult education courses given (1987, p. 13).

Increased competition from the private sector, as well as from other colleges and universities, for continuing education participants has certainly been experienced by many universities. To retain their position as a major provider of continuing education, universities must be consumer oriented. Client needs must be carefully determined; responsive programs must be designed, publicized, and presented; high standards of quality must be maintained; and positive impact must be demonstrated.

Technological Needs

New information delivery technologies, such as statewide interactive computer networks and satellite transmission capabilities, are essential for progressive extension outreach, yet are expensive to acquire, implement, and maintain. Each major technological innovation represents a substantial investment for any university. These investments must be used wisely and for the greatest public benefit.

Equal Opportunity

Cost and revenue considerations, distance, convenience, and other factors may naturally skew a university's provision of services away from some citizens, such as those who cannot pay for services or who cannot travel substantial distances. Yet many universities, particularly publicly supported ones, seek to meet the needs of all citizens, without regard to socioeconomic status, age, race, gender, religion, or mental or physical restrictions on activity. This requires periodic review of extension programming to ensure that no groups are being systematically excluded. This challenge also calls for innovative searches for funding and affirmative action to provide extension programming for those who are unable to pay.

Broad Perspectives and Specialized Resources

The trend in higher education is toward greater specialization, yet effective extension work often calls for a generalist's perspective. Extension professionals are challenged to maintain a broad perspective while also developing means to tap specialized resources to meet specific needs. Sophisticated information exchange mechanisms must be established to bring to bear specialized knowledge in a variety of contexts in meeting specific needs. Furthermore, the information network must be broad enough in scale to address local, regional, and national or international needs.

Public Awareness

The public's traditional understanding of the role of universities has emphasized undergraduate instruction and, to a lesser extent, research and graduate instruction. Some citizens are not aware of the university's extension role; in fact, some are not even aware that the Cooperative Extension Service is affiliated with land-grant universities. An important external challenge facing university extension is to broaden the public's understanding of the role of universities. Of particular concern is assisting the public to understand that universities are working to address significant community and individual concerns and needs.

Key Extension Issues to Resolve

Organizational and delivery modes, as well as the opportunities and challenges discussed above, are important considerations for university leaders involved in the creation of strategies to meet the university's extension mission. We believe there are two other key issues facing extension planners: how to train extension managers and how to reward extension programming. These are discussed briefly below.

Training Issues

Based on analysis of recent studies (for example, American Society for Training and Development, 1983; Klemp, Huff, & Gentile, 1980) and his own research, Russell (1990) suggests that extension leaders must possess, in addition to content knowledge and teaching skills, managerial abilities to: develop departmental objectives, policies, and procedures; develop and monitor budgets; recruit, select, place, appraise, and develop staff; establish positive communications systems; and solve problems and make decisions. In short, he believes extension in the 21st century will require leaders "with an entrepreneurial spirit, the ability to manage programs like any other American business enterprise, and the ability to form critical linkages between the institution, industry, and the communities they serve" (p. v).

Russell (1990) conceptualizes the extension leader of the future as an academic entrepreneur, and we agree. Some universities are developing curricula within their business schools, public administration programs, and education colleges that may produce such leaders, and some opportunities exist for continuing professional development for current extension leaders. However, we believe the creation of innovative graduate programs devoted to producing modern university extension leaders is an idea whose time has come.

Reward Issues

The age-old "law of effect" reminds us that rewarded behaviors are more likely to be repeated than those that are punished or ignored. Thus, if universities wish to have their faculties involved in extension, their reward systems must reflect this desire.

The primary rewards in academia are tenure, promotions, and salary improvements. Some universities give weight to performance in extension, outreach, and public service when making decisions about tenure, promotion, and salary adjustment; however, many do not view the extension mission as on the same level as research or instruction. These universities signal to their faculties that extension programming is a second- or third-tier activity that does not lead to high rewards; consequently, many faculty avoid extension work and concentrate on research or instruction. Still other universities give no rewards for extension; they simply provide opportunities for private consulting. In our view, this policy signals these universities' refusal to acknowledge their mission in extension.

If university extension is to flourish in the 21st century, the reward systems of many universities must be restructured to recognize excellent extension programming in their tenure, promotion, and salary adjustment policies. At present, most faculty members with cooperative extension appointments are appraised and rewarded on the basis of their plans of work. If extension is to be truly comprehensive in nature and embraced throughout a university, faculty plans of work in all units must contain extension components, and rewards must be based on excellence in extension as well as in research and instruction.

CONCLUSION

According to Derek Bok, former president of Harvard University, "Institutions can't go on enjoying the benefits of taxpayer support, and being the celebrated centers of respected learning and discovery, unless we are prepared to use those abilities in some substantial part to help the society that sustains us" ("Practical Uses," 1989, pp. 1, 4). Similarly, Norman Brown, president of the W. K. Kellogg Foundation, states, "Unprecedented efforts must be made to tap the knowledge base of the *entire* university" (1989, p. 5).

We agree with these eminent leaders in U.S. higher education, and challenge the readers of this book to join the effort to encourage our universities to attain uncharted heights in meeting our mission of comprehensive university extension in the 21st century.

NOTE

The authors thank Stephen Cosgrove, Benjamin May, Jack Smith, and Ann Thompson for reviewing earlier drafts of this chapter. We also thank all who participated in the Auburn University Extension strategic planning process for the many ideas they contributed.

REFERENCES

Alabama Cooperative Extension Service. (1987). *Priorities for people: A strategic plan for the Alabama Cooperative Extension System.* Auburn, AL: Author.

American Society for Training and Development. (1983). *Models for excellence.* Washington, DC: Author.

Armenakis, A., Burdg, H., LeNoir, C., Kuerten, K., McCord, S., & Flowers, J. (1989a). Strategic planning for consultative services organizations. *Consultation, 8*(3), 161–79.

Armenakis, A., Flowers, J. Burdg, H., Kuerten, K., McCord, S., & Arnold, D. (1989b). The business school's impact on U.S. competitiveness. *Journal of Management Development, 8*(1), 49–54.

Best, F., & Eberhard, R. (1990, May–June). Education for the "era of the adult." *Futurist, 24,* 23–28.

Brown, N. (1989, Spring). Too little, too late? *Journal of Extension, 27,* 5.

Burleson, W. C., Canup, T. W., Lambur, M. T., McAnge, T. R., Jr., Miller, M. G., Murphy, W. F., & Wolford, A. J. (1987, November 18). *Virginia Cooperative Extension Service electronic technologies and the future* (Organization Communications Committee Report, final draft). Blacksburg, VA: Virginia Cooperative Extension Service.

Caldwell, J. T. (1976). What a document . . . that land-grant act. In C. A. Vines & M. A. Anderson (Eds.), *Heritage horizons: Extension's commitment to people* (pp. 12–16). Madison, WI: Extension Journal, Inc.

Chrisman, J., Nelson, R., Hoy, F., & Robinson, R. (1985). The impact of SBDC consulting activities. *Journal of Small Business Management, 23*(3), 1–11.

Dalgaard, K., Brazzel, M., Liles, R., Sanderson, D., & Taylor-Powell, E. (1988). *Issues programming in extension.* St. Paul: Minnesota Extension Service.

Ezell, M. P. (1989, fall). Communication-age trends affecting extension: Future technological and organizational trends. *Journal of Extension, 27,* 22–24.

Futures Task Force. (1987). *Extension in transition: Bridging the gap between vision and reality.* Blacksburg, VA: Extension Committee on Organization and Policy.

Geasler, M., Bottum, J., & Patton, M. (1989). *Report of the futuring panel.* Washington, DC: Cooperative Extension System Strategic Planning Council.

Hill, S. T. (1987). *Trends in adult education, 1969–1984* (Center for Education Statistics, Office of Educational Research and Improvement, U.S. Department of Education publication). Washington, DC: U.S. Government Printing Office.

Kirkland, G. (1989). The conference center industry flexes its muscle. In *The conference center industry: A statistical and financial profile 1989* (pp. 5–7). Philadelphia: Laventhol & Horwath Hospitality Industry Consultants.

Klemp, G. O., Jr., Huff, S., & Gentile, J. G. (1980). *The guardians of campus change: A study of leadership in non-traditional college programs.* Boston: McBer and Company.

Knowlton, M. P. (1977). Liberal arts: The Elderhostel plan for survival. *Educational Gerontology, 2,* 87–93.

Meier, H. A. (1989, Fall). Extension trends and directions: Historical patterns with future necessary changes. *Journal of Extension, 27,* 11–12.

National Initiative Task Force on Youth at Risk. (1989). *Youth: The American agenda — a report of the National Initiative Task Force on Youth at Risk.* Washington, DC: U.S. Department of Agriculture Extension Services & Land-Grant University Cooperative Extension Services.

Number of adult ed participants rises dramatically. (1987, June). *Higher Education and National Affairs, 36*(11), 8.

PBS Elementary/Secondary Service. (1989). *The PBS school satellite survey.* Alexandria, VA: Author.

Practical uses for research needed to keep U.S. competitive, Bok says. (1989, January). *Higher Education and National Affairs, 38*(2), 1, 4.

Rasmussen, W. D. (1989). *Taking the university to the people: Seventy-five years of Cooperative Extension.* Ames: Iowa State.

Russell, C. (1990). *The effective management of continuing adult education in institutions of higher education.* Unpublished doctoral dissertation, Auburn University, Auburn, AL.

Sauser, W. I., Jr., Smith, E. C., & Salinger, S. F. (1982). Professionalizing Alabama county administration. *Public Sector, 5*(1 & 2).

Staffing and funding plan focuses on priorities. (1990, March). *Exclaimer, 18*(7), 2, 7.

Wilderman, J. (1989). The successful conference center. In *The conference center industry: A statistical and financial profile 1989* (p. 3). Philadelphia: Laventhol & Horwath Hospitality Industry Consultants.

12

Information Management by Colleges and Universities in the 21st Century

Boulton B. Miller

A century ago, Herman Hollerith used punched cards and a mechanical method for recording data and tabulating the 1890 U.S. census. During the past century, computers and telecommunications technologies have provided capabilities beyond most expectations. In spite of these advancements, the time has come to shift emphasis from information technology to understanding information as an organizational resource. The shift is necessary because academic information environments are changing. Strategic information and the use of information by individuals are now the major forces.

The management information systems (MIS) concept, a recognized federation of information systems and subsystems, made a major contribution. However, the MIS concept has served its purpose and it no longer provides the framework for managing information as a strategic organizational resource. The concept of information resource management (IRM) matured during the past decade. IRM originated in the federal government and is used by corporations and many others in the private sector. A few state governments, colleges, and universities use the IRM concept.

This chapter outlines specific actions for public and private academic institutions during the 1990s to prepare for 21st-century advances. Recommendations include using the IRM concept for information management and changing classroom emphasis from computer and telecommunications technology to information as an individual and organizational resource. Colleges and universities, private and public, are in an ideal position to provide leadership in this shift from an MIS environment to the IRM concept.

INFORMATION RESOURCE MANAGEMENT

Congress established the Commission on Federal Paperwork, which resulted in the enactment of the Paperwork Reduction Act of 1980 (Public Law 96-511, 96th Congress). In retrospect, this has been a major milestone toward improved information management, for the act emphasized information rather than computers and telecommunications. The results did not go unnoticed in the private sector. For example, at the McDonnell Douglas Corporation in August 1980, Ernie H. Ridenhour became one of the first to be appointed staff vice president of information resource management. A graduate course on information resource management, introduced during the 1980 fall term, was a pioneer effort. Ridenhour was mentor. The only text available for the course at that time was by Forest Woody Horton, Jr., the originator of the IRM concept. Horton drew on his work with the commission in developing the concept (Horton, 1979).

In spite of early IRM recognition demonstrated by the Ridenhour appointment, the concept lacks wide acceptance. Lack of acceptance is due to the reluctance to change and accept new concepts. The results of a study of state governments reveal that states developing an IRM approach takes several years (Caudle & Marchand, 1989).

Other needs to change emphasis are in a report from the Federal IRM Planning Support Center, U.S. General Services Administration (1989), which states that managers must be careful not to confuse the management of information technology with that of managing information, and that a well-organized automatic data processing shop does not always effectively deal with the information requirements of the entire agency.

In 1988 Peter Drucker pointed out that in the new information-based organization, there is only one conductor, the chief executive officer (CEO), and every one of the musicians plays directly to that person without intermediary. In this concept, the conductor is not expected to be able to play all the musical instructions in the orchestra. Neither is the CEO expected to be proficient in the technology of computer hardware, software, or telecommunications. As with musical instruments, the CEO, provost, or president must know whether or not the required information is provided to the right user in the desired time. The key decision for a college or university regardless of its size is to determine if the conduct of business will change as a result of a change in information processing.

INFORMATION PLANNING

The integration of information planning with strategic business planning has been slow to appear in most corporations, government agencies, and academic institutions. Until recently, information systems managers reacted to corporate business strategy planning by developing an information strategic plan to support the organization's strategic planning objectives. Most commercial planning methodologies recommend this supportive role. However, organizations should carry out a planning process that integrates information systems and business planning (Wysocki & Young, 1990).

In 1971 Milt Bryce developed the first commercial methodology recognizing the integration of planning. It is called PRIDE, the acronym for Profitable Information by Design (Bryce & Bryce, 1988). McLean and Soden pointed out the need for congruent MIS planning in 1977. The objective is that strategic planning must include information planning as well as the consideration of assets, personnel, constraints, and competition. For example, recognizing the importance of electronic data interchange (EDI) and implementing the concept can change the conduct of the business. EDI is the computer-to-computer electronic interchange of documents, such as student transcripts, between organizations in machine-readable form. Adoption of the EDI concept is a strategic management decision.

Including strategic information management planning with the organization's strategic plan is a major step in the right direction. Other steps, such as the development of computer applications, are needed to complete the IRM concept and its extension into the classroom. Under the MIS concept, information technology professionals are responsible for systems development. Under MIS leadership, end users provide limited input and little participation in systems design and development. This lack of involvement has resulted in delays, backlogs, budget overruns, and many undesirable systems.

End users, by using microcomputers, have become knowledgeable in the capabilities and limitations of information technology. End users no longer accept the decisions of MIS professionals without question. Under the IRM concept, managers and computer users assume a role of leadership in the design, development, testing, implementation, and maintenance of their computer- and telecommunications-supported systems.

It is not fair to highly talented information technology professionals that they be responsible for leadership in the development of systems they do not use. However, until functional area managers gain sufficient competence, the information systems professionals will need to continue responsibility for real-time applications and those systems that support multiple functional areas. Functional area managers as project leaders rely on information technology professionals for the technical portions of systems design and development. However, project management leadership must shift to the user community.

Principles developed by states can guide college and university planning. It is in the information management areas that statewide site licensing for student information systems and related software could be helpful. Vendors report that the states of Georgia, New Hampshire, New York, Oregon, and West Virginia use this site-licensing concept. Private institutions can receive the same benefits from state-supported principles financed by tax-generated funds.

As more state governments carry out the IRM concept, colleges and universities will gain greater support in their own efforts. However, academic institutions should take advantage of and profit from the experiences of some IRM implementations. For example, the Virginia Polytechnic Institute and State University (VPI) at Blacksburg, Virginia, implemented the IRM concept in 1983. When established, the vice president for information systems reported to the president through the senior vice president and provost of the university. Responsibilities included universitywide computing, communications (voice, video, and data), libraries, educational technology, and printing.

The system at VPI supported a single system image outlined by Robert C. Heterick, Jr. The single system image demonstrated a rethinking of an institution's commitment to information systems technology by adopting a strategic view (Heterick, 1986, 1988a, 1988b). VPI's commitment entails typical campus computer support for over 22,000 students and over 14,000 microcomputers. Many televised graduate courses are available at 10 locations around the state. The Newman Library provides technical and scientific information to the directors of technology located at the state community colleges. The system supports the VPI Extension Service with 120 offices throughout Virginia. A new centralized telecommunications equipment center, computer center, and professional personnel office building was dedicated in 1989. The location of the building, away from the central core of campus buildings, permits the facility to become the hub or focal point for information management for the entire university (Donald, 1989).

INFORMATION RESOURCE MANAGEMENT IMPLEMENTATION

Colleges and universities do not always recognize that they use a methodology for the management of information within their organizations. Information technology professionals are the primary users of the methodology, published or not. When published, the technical readability of the document is probably beyond most managers and computer users. Therefore, senior managers may not realize that a methodology exists. A common complaint in the industry is that information professionals maintain policies only for other professionals. State governments can be helpful as they adopt information resource management principles. These principles can serve as guides to private institutions as well as to the public. When these IRM principles are in place, colleges and universities can add their own, maintaining consistency with state guidelines and with each other.

The Chief Information Officer

There is a reluctance to appoint an individual as chief information office (CIO) for the management of information in colleges and universities. A 1990 study of recognized academic institutions that defined the functions of the CIO position concluded that not all colleges and universities want or need a CIO. For instance, today no more than one-third of the higher education institutions in the nation have or offer the potential for CIO positions. However, the report did identify a potential over the next decade of up to one-half of the colleges and universities in the country (Penrod, Dolence, & Douglas, 1990).

Regardless of terminology, there remains a need for an individual to provide guidance for the management of a college or university's information technology. This does not infer that the CIO should ever be an information czar, but a coordinator, a consultant, and a friend of management. As a friend, the individual, with whatever title used, serves as a confidant at all levels — top management, contemporaries, managers, and end users. However, the controversial title does not affect the reporting channel, which should be direct to the senior academic official or president of the institution.

What is important is that management makes a difference. This was the finding of a major research effort based on the specific histories of automation in seven local governmental organizations over a period of 30 years. This study identifies the actions of managers with authority over computing as the critical component of computing change. If top management does not assume this leadership role, departmental managers or management information systems directors will decide. The study brought out that many top managers avoid taking this responsibility because they believe they must become highly involved in the operational aspects of the technology. The research suggests quite the opposite, in that top management's role can be more strategic than operational (Kraemer, King, Dunkel, & Lane, 1989).

The conclusion of the Kraemer study supports these recommendations, that the provost or president remain in charge of the strategic planning to include information management, financial management, and others. The CIO or equivalent individual provides the technical inputs. However, the senior campus administrative official must fulfill for the organization what Drucker described above as the conductor, with every one of the musicians playing directly to that person.

In fulfilling this role of leadership, the senior academic officials are in ideal positions to make use of executive information systems. The fall 1989 issue of *CAUSE/EFFECT* documented interest in executive information systems and executive support systems (Viehland, 1989; Ryland, 1989). A major advantage of an executive information system is the direct involvement of the organization's top managers in the design, development, and use. These executive-level systems are no longer restricted for use by top managers. It is common to find several hundred users at various levels of the organization. Executive information systems information available on all levels of an institution will improve the decision making based on those data.

Director of Telecommunications

Most organizations have consolidated the responsibilities for voice and data, added video, graphics, and text transmission. These functions are the responsibility of the telecommunications manager. For example, on the campus of the College of William and Mary, the director of telecommunications reports to the vice provost for information technology.

The most widespread use of networks on campus is for electronic mail by administrators, faculty, and students. During the first week of class, students in an introductory MIS course send the instructor mail from their microbased terminals through a campus mainframe. By the second week the students can copy files with assignments, instructions, class notes, and chapter reference outlines, thus ending nearly all hand-outs. Campuswide voice mail is also available. Later in the course, downloading requirements permit students to move text data into word processing format, make revisions, and print the results. Downloading numeric data into spreadsheet format provides students with similar experiences.

Many campuses have replaced large transmission cables with fiber optic cable distribution systems. As a result of this rewiring, an instructor outfitted with a portable computer and projector can access the campus mainframe through a classroom cable outlet, permitting classroom demonstrations of terminal access and stand-alone microcomputer capabilities. As the cable band widths increase, graphics, images, and access to a variety of multimedia resources become available.

GET THE HOUSE IN ORDER

The discussion so far describes a base for academic institutions to begin managing information as a resource. This IRM concept includes the integration of information within strategic planning. The concept includes a senior academic position for information management or technology rather than a position as information czar. The concept includes a director of telecommunications to provide additional technical knowledge. This base, or one very similar, is in place within many academic institutions. For those not so fortunate, the foundation is a good place to begin because it serves as a platform upon which to build the remainder of the concept.

Savings are possible when state governments develop principles for colleges and universities to follow in the development of their own methodologies. For example, states can provide principles for negotiating with vendors, such as evaluation criteria for proposals received from the distribution of a request for proposal. A specific example is a microcomputer-based automated proposal evaluation spreadsheet technique developed by John W. Alwood, Department of Information Technology, Commonwealth of Virginia. The system uses electronic spreadsheets to completely automate the routine and tedious mathematics associated with the assignment of weights and points and the calculation of rankings. This permits the request for proposal evaluation and selection committee to focus on the technical, operational, and financial merits of the proposals. Computers make the computations (Alwood, 1989).

Other principles can assist in the on-line documentation of academic policies. During September 1988 a prototype example of documenting policies at the College of William and Mary was to determine whether or not an expert system shell was appropriate. The prototype documented the student financial aid policies. This proved to be a practical application for an expert system. The application resembled the use of expert system software to document coal mine safety policies that are now available worldwide (Bonnett, 1988).

State governments can establish principles to assist colleges and universities in developing their own methodologies for carrying out the IRM concept. Each college and university, private or public, large or small, has singular problems; yet, each can learn from workable solutions experienced in other institutions. State governments can identify these successes and use them as suggested principles for use by other institutions. Policies making up college and university methodologies should be documented and accessible to all, available on-line without need for printed copies or updates except to meet lingering records disposition requirements.

With this extension of state assistance, academic institutions can profit quickly from common experiences across the state. These campus-developed methodologies for information management can carry over into the classroom for use in computer-supported system instruction. Classroom instruction will profit from the advantages gained by both administrative and academic computing. Greater gains are possible where the computing resources of administrative and academic computing are consolidated. A previous study pointed out that distinctions between academic computing and administrative computing are increasingly meaningless and frustrating (Hawkins, Weissman, & Wolfe, 1989).

Records Management

The predictions of paper record reductions and paperless offices have not materialized. However, there is a need to identify those records of lasting value for retention in archives and to schedule destruction of those no longer needed. Unfortunately, the pioneer records managers and archivists did not recognize the impact computers were to have on records management. Records management programs most often omit records created electronically. State legislatures fail to include them in enough detail in their records management legislation. This failure to include electronic records was pointed out to archivists and records managers in 1965. The problem has only received minor recognition over 20 years later (Miller, 1988). Perhaps colleges and universities can assume constructive leadership in this area in the coming decade.

Data Administration

Some information technology professionals consider enterprise modeling to be a subset of data modeling. Others use an information engineering approach modeling the organization along strategic, tactical, and operational views. The PRIDE methodology, referenced above, uses an enterprise engineering methodology as a capstone to specify the duties and responsibilities of all the required functions. At this writing, lack of agreement on the methodology should not detract from the need, which is being the ability of top management to view the organization as a whole. With this view, all functional areas are identified with the data required by the processes performed. Through proper management, the data are shared and controlled, and redundancy is avoided.

An organization's data administration function is the management of all data, whether in files, in manual systems, or under data base management software. The data administrator uses a data dictionary and directory system to support the function of metadata — data about computer data. The dictionary metadata describes the data that make up the organization's computer data resources. The directory metadata describes the location and how to access the data. Another software available to the data administrator is InfoMapper for developing a base-line inventory of all information resources, internal and external (Burk & Horton, 1988).

The data administrator's function differs from that of a data base administrator, who supervises the data base management software and those data involved. A dictionary module is normally included with data base management software. The two functions for the data administrator and data base administrator are consolidated in small organizations but involve many people when several data base management software packages are in use.

The management of data in all organizations is a major concern. Problems include the lack of standardized terms, definitions, and relationships. There are many solutions, but the most appropriate is the use of an information resource dictionary system, a software system. In the federal government this system conforms to the federal information processing standard for data dictionary systems. An information resource dictionary is an application of the information resource dictionary system (Law, 1988).

Data dictionary and directory systems on college campuses provide the foundation for systems and data base design and development on all levels. At VPI, during the development work on the commercial Virginia Tech Library System in the late 1970s, university libraries became a part of the single systems image. This consolidation of information resources under the direction of the vice president for information systems is an important organizational information management arrangement. The data administrator of the future has a major responsibility.

The Division of Information Technology, Commonwealth of Virginia, recognizes the need for a strategy to develop common data element descriptions (Nelson, 1990). At Pennsylvania State University, the data administrator develops and administers policies and procedures for the management of all institutional data (Hoover, 1990). At the University of Hartford a master data dictionary serves several in support of the decision support system strategy (Glover, 1989).

Colleges and universities can profit from using information resource mapping, enterprise modeling, dictionary and directory systems, and data base management software with dictionary modules. The functions of data administrators and data base administrators need to be carried out.

Computer Instruction

Computer science departments in colleges and universities have developed a splendid reputation for providing students and graduates with outstanding technical computer instruction. The influx of foreign students in computer science classes demonstrates the global status of these programs. The over 1,200 two-year community colleges provide similar but more applications-oriented instruction. Schools of business and public administration and many other departments follow the leadership of computer science faculties by teaching computer hardware and software technology. Until the American Assembly of Collegiate Schools of Business (AACSB) introduced the Information Systems Development Institute to re-educate faculty in MIS, computer science programs provided the bulk of MIS faculty members. Other MIS faculty members, including the military, qualify through work experience.

The MIS courses recommended by the Association for Computer Machinery and the Data Processing Management Association reinforce the classroom emphasis on technology. The Porter and McKibbin study of the nation's business schools recognized improvements needed in MIS instruction (1988). Their study, sponsored by AACSB, receives little attention today. The International Foundation for Information Processing and the British Computer Society funded a similar effort to improve instruction (Buckingham, Hirscheim, Land, & Tully, 1987).

The sixth UCLA survey of business school computer usage again provided data and information on current happenings. Serious questions remain. One is of cost benefit. "It may well be that the computer is simply the typewriter and calculator of the 21st century and that our expectations for significant curriculum revision or change in the nature of instruction will not happen" (Frand & Britt, 1990). INTERACT '90: A Look into the Future of Education & Technology followed the same emphasis on technology rather than information and knowledge (INTERACT '90, 1990).

Primary and Secondary Schools

In spite of the many computers available in primary and secondary classrooms, numerous high school graduates enter college with a superficial knowledge of computers. High school graduates need an overview of the historical development of processing data to obtain information. Required practical experiences include keyboarding, using a word processor, creating spreadsheets, programming in a procedural language, and dealing with a relational data base.

Computers are valuable in most every occupation and provide an important resource in developing new areas. High school graduates can use fundamental computer understanding in many areas, even if they do not choose to enter college. This recommended requirement for high school graduates does not support the concept to emphasize information rather than technology. However, as entering the water is a basic requirement for swimming, learning to use the tools is a prerequisite for managing information.

Another tool is the ability to become information literate. Librarians lead the way toward information literacy with their traditional bibliographic instruction programs. These programs are useful in primary and secondary schools as well as in higher education. Many library professionals support a central role for the academic library similar to the integrated organization at VPI, referenced above (Euster, 1990).

Information Management Instruction

Students should realize there is a major requirement in every course for information pertinent to each discipline. Organizations are expanding into foreign markets, many in global operations. Government agencies, corporations, and other organizations have increasing interest in international data. Global business management requires information on international trade and investments as well as economic and political environments and their impact on foreign operations. Foreign data resources are more accessible by satellite transmission. Students need to realize the importance of available information resources, both internal and external, to any environment.

Computer technology has touched nearly every discipline in the humanities. Ethnomusicologists are tracing changes in jazz idioms using data bases. Literary critics can answer long-standing questions of authorship attribution with computers. Linguistics are developing strong ties with artificial intelligence. Boolean logic search techniques can find information linked by connectors — and, or, and not. For example, a library search using the Boolean technique can guide the location of every reference to a given subject in a body of text. In the past some scholars spent much of their scholarly lives compiling concordances — alphabetical indexes of the principal words in a book or the works of an author. A computer can now duplicate these efforts in a matter of minutes. In summary, the use of computers in humanities research encourages the spread of interdisciplinary research (Raymond, 1989). The 1990 *Tyrannical Machines* report from the National Endowment for the Humanities provides new documentation (Cheney, 1990).

Colleges and universities have numerous computer applications supporting administrative functions. Any number of these applications can provide excellent classroom examples of information technology. For instance, a student information system, whether purchased from a vendor or developed in-house, can provide a teaching vehicle for a classroom evaluation and education. A typical commercial student information system software package provides the user with a report generation capability, often a fourth generation language (4GL). A 4GL is a software package, rather than a programming language like COBOL, and may be available under a sole-source agreement.

When this 4GL software becomes available, the vendor usually supplies a mainframe version of the software for academic use in the classroom without charge. This provides the faculty with a resource to use with students in developing applications usable by administrative staff as well as academic units.

One instructor began using a PC-based 4GL package in 1983 to maintain information on all students in assigned classes. The students enter their personal information on the professor's system. This gives them an understanding of data entry, a chance to see where their mail to the instructor arrives, and an opportunity for questions and one-on-one interaction.

The 4GL software is available for use by student teams to develop work group applications, which give the students an understanding of software capabilities and limitations. The student teams design and organize small data bases and automatically generate 4GL code, which adds, displays, updates, and deletes data. Students need to see before believing that 300 or 400 lines of 4GL programming code is developed in 12 to 15 seconds.

Students seem to enjoy developing reports because of their previous experiences with procedural programming languages. Students learn best by doing something on their own. In this case, the students learn more from giving their own instructions to the computer to perform sorts for report generation. They can see for themselves how to produce a list of all team members in numerical team order. With the addition of minor instruction, a new listing arranges the team members in alphabetical order. The project team work is menu driven, requiring the students to spend an hour or less completing the initial assignment to develop a similar application.

Some project teams go beyond the course requirement through study of the 4GL user manual. With little guidance, the teams expand their applications beyond the expectations of an introductory course. Many of these more ambitious students find employment with vendors as consultants, or with corporations, government agencies, or academic institutions. This instruction serves as an introduction to an advanced course in data base design and management. The campus data base administrator is a resource seldom used to teach this data base course.

Systems Development

Systems development life-cycle methodology describes applications development. The systems development life-cycle nomenclature is avoided by some who point out that systems do not have a life cycle, only projects do ("What's in a Word?" 1990). More than one methodology is often necessary because of the differences in development. To some this is a difference in technique rather than in methodology. However, there are differences when a request for a proposal is used. Applications developed completely in-house also differ. Users are more involved as members of joint applications development teams.

Some organizations will subscribe to commercial methodologies from such vendors as Andersen Consulting, Bachman Information Systems, IBM, KnowledgeWare, McDonnell Douglas Corporation, or Texas Instruments. Others will use the PRIDE system engineering product and methodology, including the Information Factory, to simulate a manufacturing environment. Whatever methodologies are used, documentation is a necessity, preferably by using computer-aided systems or software engineering (CASE) tools.

CASE tools for student use, in their present design have limited application because of the learning curves. However, for classroom demonstration purposes, CASE tools are useful to show data flows, processes, and storage requirements. At the graduate level, when a computer-supported application meets the requirement of a thesis, the student can make full use of the CASE technology. Three faculty members witness the student-developed application to insure proper design. This practical application of classroom instruction becomes useful résumé reference material for the students.

CASE tools included in systems development methodologies provide improved documentation and can make automatic updates when changes are necessary. Usage will pay for the investment. Special CASE tools can provide enhancement or re-engineering of old applications. These tools are important because of the typical maintenance backlogs found in most organizations (Ricketts, 1990). At this writing, a leading re-engineering contributor in the information industry is Charles W. Bachman, CEO of Bachman Information systems. IBM included the Bachman company as one of three vendor software firms making up an inner circle of supporters for its AD/Cycle concept.

Application and Maintenance Backlogs

Unfortunately, academic institutions suffer from backlogs in application development and maintenance similar to those found in corporations and government agencies. The fall of the average corporate backlog from 33 months to 29 months between 1986 and 1989 indicated minor improvement (Newsfront, 1990). CASE tools, 4GLs, and improved methodologies deserve some credit. However, excessive backlogs should not be acceptable in any organization. Many users expend efforts on their own microcomputer applications rather than mainframe backlogs.

A solution for the reduction of application and maintenance backlogs is for users to be responsible for operating and maintaining their own computer applications. This concept magnifies a user's most important asset, which is knowing more than anyone else about the data and the information required from the data. This concept has been in use at VPI for several years (Donald, 1989).

The introduction of a 4GL at Yale University in 1979 provided a similar backlog reduction. The important factor in reducing the backlog is a well-trained user community willing to generate his or her own applications (Johnson, 1989, 1990).

CONCLUSION

Colleges and universities need to shift the current emphasis on computers and telecommunications technology to the importance of information as a resource. This shift requires the development of a methodology for the management of information as an important institutional resource. This assumes that state governments have implemented the IRM concept and developed principles that will assist the development of private and public campus methodologies. Another asset is the consolidation of administrative and academic computing. Other steps are to include some form of enterprise modeling, institutionwide data administration using some form of base-line inventory of all information resources, a dictionary and directory system, and an executive information system. The campus reference librarian should become the de facto campus data administrator for the college or university, supervising data base administrators and distributed campus library data administrators. Using data base management systems and methodologies for the design, development, testing, implementation, maintenance, and re-engineering of computer applications are necessary.

A major requirement is that all students entering college take a course stressing the importance of information as a source of knowledge. This required course redirects the emphasis in typical computer concepts courses. It assumes that high school graduates have knowledge of word processing, spreadsheets, relational data bases, and programming, and that they are information literate, not just computer literate.

The next recommendation is for each discipline or area of study to build on the required introductory knowledge acquisition course.

The information requirements, resources, and software necessary for each discipline requires identification and use. For example, accounting majors need the introductory information course before learning about accounting systems and software support. The same emphasis is expected in each academic area.

With this foundation, college and universities can take advantage of the advances anticipated during the 21st century. Without this foundation, students will lack the appreciation of information as a resource and the ability to obtain the necessary knowledge for improved decisions.

REFERENCES

Alwood, J. W. (1989, September 7). Letter to Boulton B. Miller. (Note: The copyright for the methodology is held by the Commonwealth of Virginia; the author is John W. Alwood, Computer Systems Chief Engineer, Division of Telecommunications, Department of Information Technology, Commonwealth of Virginia, Richmond, VA.)

Bonnett, K. (1988). *U.S. Bureau of Mines' expert systems keep coal mines safer worldwide*. New York: Information Builders.

Bryce, M., & Bryce, T. (1988). *The IRM revolution: Blueprint for the 21st century*. Palm Harbor, FL: M. Bryce & Associates.

Buckingham, R. A., Hirscheim, R. A., Land, F. F., and Tully, C. J. (Eds.). (1987). *Information systems education*. Cambridge: Cambridge University Press on behalf of the British Computer Society.

Burk, C. F., Jr., & Forest W. Horton, Jr. (1988). *InfoMap: A complete guide to discovering corporate information resources*. Englewood Cliffs, NJ: Prentice-Hall. (InfoMapper software is a product of Information Management Press, Washington, DC.)

Caudle, S. L., & Marchand, D. A. (1989, August). *Managing information resources: New directions in state government*. Syracuse, NY: Syracuse University, Center for Science and Technology.

Cheney, L. V. (1990). *Tyrannical machines* (Report). Washington, DC: National Endowment for the Humanities.

Donald, A. W. (1989, August 4). Assistant Vice President Information Systems. Interview with the author, Virginia Polytechnic Institute and State University, Blacksburg, VA.

Drucker, P. (1988, January–February). The coming of the new organization. *Harvard Business Review, 66*(1), 45–53.

Euster, J. R. (1990, Winter). Review of P. S. Breivik and E. G. Gee, *Information literacy: Revolution in the library. CAUSE/EFFECT, 13*(4), 54.

Federal IRM Planning Support Center. (1989). *The IRM organization: Concepts and considerations*. Washington, DC: U.S. General Services Administration, Office of Software Development and Information Technology.

Frand, J. L., & Britt, J. A. (1990). Sixth annual UCLA survey of business school computer usage. *Communications of the ACM, 33*(5), 562.

Glover, R. H. (1989). Decision support/executive systems at the University of Hartford. *CAUSE/EFFECT, 12*(3), 19.

Gongla, P., Sakamoto, G., Back-Hock, A., Goldweic, P., Ramos, L., Sprowls, R. C., & Kim, C. K. (1989). S*P*A*R*K: A knowledge-based system for identifying competitive uses of information technology. *IBM Systems Journal, 28*(4), 628–45.

Goodhue, D. L., Quillard, J. A., & Rockart, J. F. (1988, September). Managing the data resource: A contingency perspective. *MIS Quarterly,* 373–92.

Hawkins, B. L., Weissman, R. F. E., & Wolfe, D. C. (1989). Prescriptions for managing information resources on campus. In B. L. Hawkins (Ed.), *Organizing and managing information resources on campus* (p. 249). McKinney, TX: EDUCOM and Academic Computing Publications.

Heterick, R. C., Jr. (1986). An information systems strategy. *CAUSE/EFFECT, 9*(6), 13.

____. (1988a, January). *Information systems: A planning prospectus.* Blacksburg, VA: Virginia Polytechnic Institute & State University.

____. (1988b). *A single system image: An information systems strategy.* Boulder, CO: CAUSE.

Hoover, R. G. (1990, Winter). Data administration at Penn State: Problems and solutions. *CAUSE/EFFECT, 13*(4), 41–46.

Horton, F. W., Jr. (1979). *Information resources management: Concept and cases.* Cleveland, OH: Association for Systems Management.

INTERACT '90. (1990, May 10). A look into the future of education and technology. A satellite conference from California State University, Chico, at the College of William and Mary, Williamsburg, VA.

Johnson, M. (1989, December–January). Drowning in a sea of code. *Computerworld, 25,* 10.

Kraemer, K. L., King, J. L., Dunkle, D. E., & Lane, J. P. (1989). *Managing information systems change and control in organizational computing.* San Francisco: Jossey-Bass Publishers.

Law, M. H. (1988). *Guide to information resource dictionary system applications: General concepts and strategic systems planning* (NBS Special Publication 500-152). Washington, DC: Department of Commerce, National Bureau of Standards.

McLean, E., & Soden, J. V. (1977). *Strategic planning for MIS.* New York: John Wiley & Sons.

Miller, B. B. (1988). Managing information as a resource. In J. Rabin & E. M. Jacowski (Eds.), *Handbook of information resource management* (pp. 3–33). New York: Marcel Dekker.

Nelson, J. A. (Ed.). (1990, March). Virginia's use and management of information technology. In J. A. Nelson (Ed.), *Gateways to comprehensive state information policy* (pp. 106–10). Lexington, KY: Chief Officers of State Library Agencies and the Council of State Governments.

Newsfront. (1990, March). Backlog still flat at 29 months. *Software Magazine* (International Ed.), *10*(3), 12.

Penrod, J. I., Dolence, M. G., & Douglas, J. V. (1990). *The chief information officer in higher education.* Professional Paper Series, #4. Boulder, CO: CAUSE, Appendix /27.

Porter, L. W., & McKibbin, L. E. (1988). *Management education and development.* New York: McGraw-Hill.

Raymond, C. (1989, July 12). Humanities researchers experience a "sea of change" in the use of computers in their disciplines. *Chronicle of Higher Education, 35,* A6, A24.

Ricketts, J. (1990). Information systems renovation. In A. Milton Jenkins, H. S. Seigle, W. Wojtkowski, & W. G. Wjotkowski (Eds.), *Research issues in information systems: An agenda for the 1990s* (pp. 193–216). Dubuque, IA: Wm. C. Brown Publishers.

Ryland, J. N. (1989). An interview with John F. Rockart. *CAUSE/EFFECT, 12*(3), 9.

Viehland, D. W. (1989). Executive information systems in higher education. *CAUSE/EFFECT, 12*(3), 7.

What's in a Word? (1990, April). *Management Visions, 6*(2), 5. (A newsletter.) Palm Harbor, FL: M. Bryce & Associates.

Wysocki, R. K., & Young, J. (1990). *Information systems: Management principles in action.* New York: John Wiley & Sons.

Bibliographic Essay

Managing Institutions of Higher Education into the 21st Century: Issues and Implications (MIHE 21C) is intended to help institutions of higher education determine now what must be done to improve their management and insure their survival as they move into the 21st century. With this in mind, a key question one should ask is: How is this book different from the current literature on this topic? This essay briefly discusses four books that comprise the key current and relevant literature addressing higher education issues.

New Priorities for the University by Ernest Lynton and Sandra Ellman is similar to MIHE 21C in that it identifies several important issues for higher education as they relate to the role and function of higher education in a changing society. Lynton and Ellman present a well-written text that focuses the reader's attention on several diverse areas as they apply to the modern university's attempt to "meet society's needs for applied knowledge and competent individuals" (p. xii). It is our belief that MIHE 21C differs from *New Priorities* in two ways: First, MIHE 21C identifies and discusses a larger variety of issues that institutions of higher education must face in the future. Second, the chapters of MIHE 21C are written by specialists in each area.

George Keller's *Academic Strategy* introduces the concept of strategic planning as it can be applied to institutions of higher education. However, Keller's discussion fails to tie the concept of strategic planning into specific situations or examples with which institutions of higher education will be faced, presently or in the future. As a result Keller's book cannot serve as a good reference book for college presidents, administrators, higher education faculty, or students interested in using strategic planning to find solutions to current and future problems or to foresee future problems and potential opportunities. In addition, although correct in identifying an important management technique (strategic planning) that institutions of higher education must employ in order to be competitive and survive, it does not go far enough. *Academic Strategy* could serve as a supplemental reader for MIHE 21C.

Lewis B. Mayhew's *Surviving the Eighties* looks primarily at solving fiscal and enrollment problems. It is an excellent text but very limited in scope. Mayhew contends that institutions of higher education must look beyond the limited scope of fiscal and enrollment problems, which is the very intent of the more complex structure in MIHE 21C. MIHE 21C not only looks at these problems but incorporates numerous responses to future and present problems as they relate to the governance and administration of institutions of higher education, academic considerations, service and outreach, and research and technology.

Finally, *Three Thousand Futures* by the Carnegie Council on Policy Studies in Higher Education primarily offers a checklist of problems of which institutions of higher education and state and federal governments must be aware over a 20-year span. *Three Thousand Futures* is very comprehensive in identifying problems but offers little in the way of solutions, while MIHE 21C provides readers with practical outlines and action steps and, where appropriate, designates who should be responsible for managing recommended changes in colleges and universities.

Index

About the Contributors

Richard E. Boyatzis is professor of organizational behavior at Weatherhead School of Management, Case Western Reserve University. He earned his Ph.D. from Harvard University in social psychology. His principal research interests involve competencies, integrated human resource management systems, management of professional service firms, and social and cultural context behavior. He is the author of *The Competent Manager.*

Norman J. Bregman is assistant vice president for academic affairs at Butler University. He was an American Council on Education Fellow 87–88 at George Mason University. He has published articles on psychology and the law, biofeedback, and interpersonal attraction.

Hugh M. Cannon is the Adcraft/Simons-Michelson professor of marketing at Wayne State University. He holds Ph.D., M.Phil., and M.B.A. degrees in marketing and organizational behavior from New York University and an A.B. degree from Brigham Young University. He has published more than 70 scholarly articles and monographs relating to marketing and education. He is an active consultant and is a member of several national associations, including the Association for Business Simulations and Experiential Learning, of which he is vice president and executive director. His current research interests include methods of strategy development and how decision makers organize and use knowledge.

Arthur W. Chickering is professor of leadership and human development at George Mason University. He completed his Ph.D. in school psychology at Teachers College, Columbia University. He was distinguished professor and director of the Center for Higher Education at Memphis State University from 1977–88. An expert on educational practices, college environments, and student development, Chickering has received many honors. He is the author of *Education and Identity, Commuting vs. Resident Students, Experience and Learning, The Modern American College,* and *Improving Higher Education Environments for Adults.*

Scott S. Cowen is professor of accountancy and dean at the Weatherhead School of Management, Case Western Reserve University. He received his doctorate in accounting from George Washington University. His research interests are in management and cost accounting and management control.

Russell W. Driver is associate dean and associate professor of management, College of Business Administration, University of Oklahoma. As associate dean he is responsible for all internal functioning of the college. He has over 20 years of administrative and management experience in nonacademic organizations. Among the clients for whom he has provided consultation are Firestone, Goodyear, Honeywell, and American Motors. His Ph.D. in business is from the University of Georgia, where he majored in organizational behavior. He has published extensively in both academic and professional journals.

Betty Duvall is executive dean of the Rock Creek Campus, Portland Community College. She holds a Ph.D. from St. Louis University, an M.A. from New York University in humanities, and an M.A. in librarianship from the University of Denver. She has served as president of the National Council of Instructional Administrators, an affiliated council of ASCJC. She has served as a consultant and evaluator for the Northwest and North Central Regional Accrediting agencies and has been a frequent speaker on issues relating to community college instruction.

Ralph S. Foster, Jr., is project associate in the office of the vice president for extension at Auburn University. He received his B.S. in business administration marketing from Auburn University and his M.S. in personnel management from Troy State University. He is a member of the International Board of Directors of the Society for Advancement of Management and is a fellow of the society. He also serves on the Region VII program committee of the Association for Continuing Higher Education.

Roberto P. Haro is a Mexican-American academician who has served in different capacities in higher education. He earned his doctorate from the University of California at Berkeley in organizational development, policy studies, and higher education administration. He is currently professor of Mexican-American studies and director of the Monterey County Campus of San Jose State University. He has worked and taught at the University of California, the State University of New York, the University of Maryland, and the University of Southern California. Haro was an American Council on Education fellow in 1987–88, is a frequent contributor to the professional literature in several fields, and has published 5 monographs and over 50 articles and chapters.

William T. Henwood has more than 22 years of administrative and management experience in large organizations. For more than two years he has been director of administration and operations, College of Business Administration, University of Oklahoma. He has enjoyed numerous successes as a change agent and team builder in organizations.

James T. Kenny is vice chancellor for research and development at Auburn University at Montgomery. He chairs that institution's Research Council and has worked in the organization of cooperative university, corporate, and governmental programs.

David A. Kolb is professor of organizational behavior at the Weatherhead School of Management, Case Western Reserve University. His principal research interests are individual and social change, experiential learning, career development, and executive and professional education. With his extensive academic background and research on experiential learning he has become a recognized authority in the field of experiential learning. He is the author of *Experiential Learning: Experience as a Source of Learning and Development.*

Sonia R. Livingston is a research specialist in the Center for Business and Economic Development, Auburn University at Montgomery, where she is responsible for conducting job analyses, constructing and administering organizational questionnaires, and developing job knowledge test items, oral interview questions, and assessment center exercises. She received her B.A. in English from Auburn University.

Boulton B. Miller is a visiting professor in information systems at the School of Business Administration, College of William and Mary. He received his Ph.D. in public administration from

American University. Miller is a retired colonel in the U.S. Army, where his involvement with computers and management information systems grew out of the need for support of U.S. Army troops in the field. His interests are in the management of information resources.

Micheal R. Moffett is professor and dean of education, Southeastern Louisiana University. He has held several administrative assignments in higher education and specializes in educational management and administration.

J. R. Morris is Regents' Professor of psychology and higher education at the University of Oklahoma, where he has served as provost and senior vice president. He is a clinical psychologist with a Ph.D. from the University of Oklahoma. In 1987, he returned to teaching after having completed 25 years in academic administration. He currently directs the doctoral program in higher education administration.

David Potter presently holds the position of vice president for executive affairs at George Mason University. Previously he was assistant director for academic programs at the State Council for Higher Education for Virginia and was a fellow in academic administration of the American Council on Education. For nine years he taught anthropology and urban studies at Denison University, where he also served as chair of the Department of Sociology and Anthropology and as director of the Urban Studies Program. He completed his doctoral work at the Maxwell School of Citizenship and Public Affairs, Syracuse University, majoring in social science with emphasis on anthropology and a concentration in Southeast Asia.

William I. Sauser, Jr., Ph.D., is associate vice president for extension and professor of educational foundations, leadership, and technology at Auburn University. He earned his B.S. in management and M.S. and Ph.D. in Industrial/Organizational Psychology at Georgia Institute of Technology. Dr. Sauser is a past president of the Alabama Psychological Association and is international president-elect of the Society for Advancement of Management. He is also a 1991–92 American Council on Education Fellow.

Ronald R. Sims is associate professor of business administration at the College of William and Mary. He has been concerned primarily with employee and management development, experiential learning, and organizational change and effectiveness. He is the author of *An Experiential Learning Approach to Employee*

Behavior, and has written extensively for scholarly and practitioner-oriented journals.

Serbrenia J. Sims earned her Ed.D. in higher education administration from the College of William and Mary. Her research interests are in student assessment and institutional effectiveness. She has co-authored several articles on the ethics of higher education and increasing partnerships between business school and corporations. She is the author of *Student Outcomes Assessment: A Historical Review and Guide to Program Development.*

John G. Veres III is director of the Center for Business and Economic Development at Auburn University at Montgomery. He received his Ph.D. in industrial/organizational psychology from Auburn University. His primary interests include personnel administration, equal employment opportunity, the development and validation of employee selection procedures, the design of performance appraisal systems, and other human resource management applications. He has written extensively in scholarly journals, having published over 30 papers and book chapters in the areas of human resource management.

Raymond B. Wells is director of the Center for Government and Public Affairs and an associate professor, Department of Political Science and Public Administration, Auburn University at Montgomery. Previously he was assistant director of finance for the state of Alabama, with a dual capacity as state budget officer. He is chair of the Information Systems Task Force for the state of Alabama and is also responsible for major new systems development activities in financial management systems at the Department of Human Resources and the Department of Mental Health and Mental Retardation. He received his Ph.D. in political science from Texas Tech University.

Lawrence Wiseman is professor and chair, Department of Biology, College of William and Mary. He received his Ph.D. from Princeton University, has been a National Cancer Institute Fellow, and served on staff in the Human Leukemia Program, Ontario Cancer Institute. He was an American Council on Education Fellow and special assistant to the president at the University of Colorado during the academic year 1987–88. He has authored or co-authored more than two dozen papers and abstracts on cellular and developmental biology, and a half dozen papers on college athletics and other subjects. He recently co-authored *The Old College Try: Balancing Academics and Athletics in Higher Education.* He is a charter, elected member of the Faculty Assembly at William and Mary, and former chair of the Athletic Policy Advisory Committee and faculty representative to the National Collegiate Athletic Association.